HISTORY ★ THROUGH ★ FILM
WITH
BRITISH PATHÉ

Why Remember
the First World War?

PAUL TURNER

OXFORD
UNIVERSITY PRESS

OXFORD
UNIVERSITY PRESS

Great Clarendon Street, Oxford, OX2 6DP, United Kingdom

Oxford University Press is a department of the University of Oxford. It furthers the University's objective of excellence in research, scholarship, and education by publishing worldwide. Oxford is a registered trade mark of Oxford University Press in the UK and in certain other countries

British Library Cataloguing in Publication Data
Data available

978-0-19-830758-7

10 9 8 7 6 5 4 3 2

MIX
Paper from
responsible sources
FSC® C007785

Paper used in the production of this book is a natural, recyclable product made from wood grown in sustainable forests.
The manufacturing process conforms to the environmental regulations of the country of origin.

Printed in Great Britain by Bell and Bain Ltd, Glasgow

Acknowledgements

The publisher and the authors would like to thank the following for permissions to use their photographs:

Cover: Hulton-Deutsch Collection/CORBIS; Karina Bakalyan/ Shutterstock

p4: AEPhotographic/Shutterstock; p5: ngelo Hornak/Corbis; p6: Leonard de Selva/ Corbis; p12: Hulton-Deutsch Collection/CORBIS; p13: Imperial War Museum; p14: Mary Evans Picture Library/Onslow Auctions Limited; p15: Swim Ink 2, LLC/ CORBIS; p15: Corbis; p15: Heritage Images/Corbis; p16: Imperial War Museum; p16: Popperfoto/Getty images; p19: Getty Images/Popperfoto; p21: www. ww1battlefields.co.uk; p23: Museum of London; p24: Bettmann/CORBIS; p26: Science Photo Library/National Museum of Health and Medicine; p.31: Karyn Mooney; p32: NTERFOTO / Alamy; p33: The Art Archive / Alamy; p35: IWM/Getty Images; p36: Getty Images/Hulton Archive; p36: Haig Master of the Sword by Sir John H Davidson/Pen & Sword Books; p37: Punch; p39: jaxpix / Alamy; p40: Getty Images/Hulton Archive; p40: Mary Evans Picture Library; p40: Illustrated London News Ltd/Mary Evans; p41: Mary Evans Picture Library; p44: Getty Images; p47: IWM via Getty Images; p47: Bettmann/CORBIS; p48: Hulton-Deutsch Collection/ CORBIS; p48: From the Archives of the Royal College of Surgeons of England; p50: IWM via Getty Images; p51: Bettmann/CORBIS; p51: Popperfoto/Getty Images; p52: The Print Collector / Alamy; p52: Mary Evans Picture Library/Pump Park Photography; p53: PUNCH;
p54: Getty Images.

OUP would also like to thank British Pathé for permission to use still images from their films throughout this book.

Illustrations: Rudolf Farkas and Martin Sanders

From the author, Paul Turner: To Claire, William, Henry and Mollie. This book is dedicated to you, my family, who have supported me through many late evenings and frustrating weekends when I have been working on this project. Without you I would have no inspiration. I would also like to thank Sarah Flynn for giving me this opportunity and Lois Durrant for being so upbeat and positive about what I have written.

OUP wishes to thank Kevin Newman, Head of History at Downlands Community School, and Alf Wilkinson, for their help reviewing, and contributing to, this book.

We would also like to thank the students of Downlands Community School for their help trialling our resources and making helpful suggestions.

We are grateful to the following for permission to reprint copyright material.

Australian War Memorial for article about the Anzac Day Ceremony, copyright © Australian War Memorial, from www.awn.gov.au/anzac/anzactradition.

BBC for extracts from the History website, www.bbc.co.uk/history: 'The Pals Battalions in World War One' by Bruce Robinson, 3.10.2011; 'India and the Western Front by David Omissi', 3.10.2011; and Arthur Barraclough account at 'Over the Top' from The Last Tommy Gallery.

Bloomsbury Publishing plc for extracts from The Last Fighting Tommy by Harry Patch with Richard Van Emden (Bloomsbury, 2008), copyright © Harry Patch and Richard Van Emden 2008; and Boy Soldiers of the Great War by Richard Van Emden (Bloomsbury, 2012), copyright © Richard Van Emden 2012.

Commonwealth War Graves Commission for extract from Forever India story: 'Khudadad Khan and Ghulam Haider' from www.cwgc.org/foreverindia.

Constable & Robinson for extract from Dive! Dive! Dive! Submarines at War by Michael Gunton (Constable, 2003).

Dorling Kindersley for extract from World War 1 by H P Willmott (2e, 2012), copyright © Dorling Kindersley Ltd 2008.

Guardian News & Media Ltd for extract from 'The brothers who made a stand' by Sabine Durrant, The Guardian, 8.11.2008, copyright © Guardian News and Media Ltd 2008.

David Omissi for 'India and the Western Front' BBC History website, 3.10.2011.

Elena Lester, The History Blog for extract from 'Manchester's sewer-building heroes of WW1', www.thehistoryblog.com.

Penguin Books Ltd for extract from The First World War: An Illustrated History by A J P Taylor (Hamish Hamilton, 1963, 1966, 1974), copyright © George Rainbird Ltd, 1963.

The Random House Group Ltd for extracts from Forgotten Voices of The Great War by Max Arthur (Ebury Press, 2002, 2006); The Unknown Soldier by Neil Hanson (Doubleday 2005/Corgi 2007); and Forgotten Voices of the Somme by Joshua Levine (Ebury Press, 2008).

Royal Society of Medicine for extract from media release, 1 Sept 2006, re 'The life and death of Private Harry Farr' by Simon Wessely, Journal of the Royal Society of Medicine, Vol 99 (Sept, 2006), http://jrs.sagepub.com/content/99/9/440.full.http:// jrs.sagepub.com/content/99/9/440.full.

The Telegraph Media Group for extracts from 'Secret Terror weapon of the Somme battle discovered' by Jasper Copping, The Telegraph, 9.5.2010, copyright © Telegraph Media Group Ltd 2010; 'How we should remember the First World War' by Harry Mount, The Telegraph, 96.2013, copyright © Telegraph Media Group Ltd 2013; 'Pardoned, the 306 soldiers shot at dawn for cowardice' by Ben Fenton, The Telegraph, 16.8.2006, copyright © Telegraph Media Group Ltd 2006; and 'Boy 12 was the youngest British soldier in First World War' by Julie Henry, The Telegraph, 31.10.2009, copyright © Telegraph Media Group Ltd 2009.

Jim Tothill for extract from the Roxburgh Diaries, his father's WW1 naval journal, 18 July 1917, www.jimtothill.com/roxburgh.

Western Front Association and the author for extract from 'Shell Shock: Genesis and Outcomes in the Great War' by Dr David Payne, 22.5.2008, www.westernfrontassociation.com

We have made every effort to trace and contact all copyright holders before publication, but if notified of any errors or omissions, the publisher will by happy to rectify these at the earliest opportunity.

Links to digital resources
Whenever you see this film icon in the book, it means that there is a relevant film and accompanying film worksheet on *Kerboodle*. These resources have been produced in partnership with British Pathé.

Contents

1.1 The Great War today

OBJECTIVES
- Identify ways in which the First World War is remembered.
- State why it is important to remember the war.
- Explain the possible consequences of not remembering the war.

SOURCE B: The Queen Mother laying a cross in the Garden of Remembrance, London, 1964.

SOURCE A: Tyne Cot military cemetery, Belgium.

Look at **Source A**. What do you see? Thousands of people visit places like this every year – you may even have had the chance to go yourself. These are the graves of those who lost their lives on the **battlefields** of the First World War. The First World War was the first truly **global** war. No war before it had been of such scale or resulted in such loss of life. No war before it had seen so many new tactics and so many new weapons.

Visiting the battlefields today involves travelling through the flat, green farmland of France and Belgium, taking in the fresh country air, far from the troubles that the soldiers, nurses and orderlies had to endure during the conflict. How do you think you would feel visiting the sites of such famous and historic battles?

KEY FIRST WORLD WAR SITES ON THE WESTERN FRONT

Name of site	What can be found there?
Langemarck, Belgium	Flat gravestones mark shared German graves.
Sanctuary Wood, Belgium	Examples of trenches and artefacts connected to the war.
Lochnagar crater at La Boiselle, France	Huge crater caused by a mine – 300ft wide, 70ft deep (90 × 20m).
Menin Gate, Belgium	At 8pm every day 'The Last Post' is sounded.
Thiepval, France	Memorial to those missing on the Somme.
Ypres, Belgium	Medieval town that was heavily damaged in the fighting. Now restored, it welcomes visitors from around the globe to remember the war.
Ulster Tower, France	**Memorial** to the Irish soldiers who fought on the Somme (the 36th Ulster division).
Tyne Cot, Belgium	11,956 burials; 8369 unidentified. Largest war graves site in the world.
Cobbers Memorial, France	Sculpture at Fromelles – dedicated to Australian troops.

 KEY WORDS

battlefields
global
memorial
Western Front

STOP THE CLOCK

4 August 2014 marks the 100th anniversary of the start of the First World War.

WHY SHOULD WE STILL VISIT THE BATTLEFIELDS?

It keeps the war in living memory.

The battlefields are a unique insight into the war.

It reminds us of the debt that we owe to those who fought.

You can conduct your own, first-hand research into the war.

It brings trade and revenue to various nations.

Artefacts and relics are not lost over time.

Seeing the size of the battlefields helps us comprehend the scale of loss.

The First World War touched every village and town in Britain. Millions served and almost 900,000 United Kingdom subjects died in action. The loss to this country and to countless families was unimaginable and must not be forgotten. That is why it is important that a new generation should be encouraged to remember the sacrifice of so many.

SOURCE C: Comments about the First World War from the Education Secretary, Michael Gove, June 2013.

 TASKS

1 a   Where are the **Western Front** battlefields of the First World War?
   b   Why do people visit them?
2 Read the speech bubbles which give reasons for why people should visit the battlefields.
   a   Put them in order of importance (remember that this is your opinion).
   b   Add any more reasons you can think of.
3 Read **Source C**.
   a   What reasons does Michael Gove give for why we should remember the First World War?
   b   Could you extend his argument to make it more convincing? Use the reasons in task **2**.
4 Using what you've learned in this lesson, EITHER:
   a   design a poster that aims to persuade people to visit the battlefields OR
   b   write a letter to the 'Unknown Soldier', explaining what has been done to commemorate his sacrifice, and why.
5 Put together a short guide to the battlefields of the First World War using the sites mentioned on these pages. You will need to use the Internet to help you with this.

PEOPLE OF WWI

The 'Unknown Soldier' was buried on 11 November 1920 to commemorate all those who served and gave their lives for their country.

SOURCE D: The tombstone of the Unknown Soldier in Westminster Abbey.

FINAL FOCUS

Remembering a war may not prevent similar wars from happening again, but it keeps it at the front of our minds. Do you think this is important? Why?

SOURCE A: An illustration in *Le Paris Journal* showing the assassination of the Archduke and his wife in 1914.

STOP THE CLOCK

28 June 1914 – The Archduke Franz Ferdinand and his wife Sophie were assassinated by Gavrilo Princip, in Sarajevo.

Today we live in a world where every event or action that could lead to war is reported in great detail. Yet the world's leaders seem to take an age to make a decision about whether to wage war. Perhaps this is because nobody really wants war. Would you expect your country to go to war over a small, seemingly unimportant event?

FROM MURDER TO WAR

Such an event occurred on 28 June 1914, when a young Serbian man named Gavrilo Princip fired his pistol three times. At only 19 years of age he cannot have expected that his actions would have had such big consequences. The shots that murdered Archduke Franz Ferdinand, the heir to the Austro-Hungarian throne, and his wife Sophie, set off a chain of events that led to the outbreak of the First World War. Yet Gavrilo Princip had not been the only terrorist on the streets of Sarajevo on that unfortunate day. So why did fate lie in his hands?

SOURCE B: The Archduke Franz Ferdinand and his wife Sophie.

PEOPLE OF WWI: GAVRILO PRINCIP

Why was he trying to kill the Archduke?
His country, Serbia, had been taken over by the Austro-Hungarian Empire, but they wanted to rule themselves. This was an act of protest. He thought that killing the heir to the throne would make them think again about Serbia.

What was the name of his organization?
It was called the **Black Hand gang**.

Is it true that somebody else had failed to kill him?
Yes – Princip's compatriot Cabrinovic had thrown a bomb at the car but it had not been successful.

Was he the only person trying to kill him?
He was one of seven terrorists on the day, all with the same aim.

SOURCE D: Gavrilo Princip.

Why was the Archduke visiting the city?
To inspect the Austrian troops based in the city and to attend an official function.

Was the Archduke his only target?
Yes – it was apparently not his intention to kill the Archduke's wife Sophie as well.

> When the car arrived I recognized the Heir ... but as I saw a lady sitting next to him I reflected for a moment whether I should shoot or not. At the same moment I was filled with a peculiar feeling and I aimed at the Heir Apparent from the pavement – which was made easier because the car was proceeding slower at that moment. Where I aimed I do not know. But I know that I aimed at the Heir Apparent. I believe that I fired twice, perhaps more because I was so excited. Whether I hit the victim or not, I cannot tell, because instantly people turned around to hit me.

SOURCE C: Gavrilo Princip's description of what happened on 28 June 1914.

TASKS

1. a When did the assassination take place?
    b What was the name of the terrorist organization?
    c Who was the target of the assassination?
2. Using the details given about Gavrilo Princip on this page, explain the assassination from his point of view – did he believe that he was doing the right thing?
3. Write or act out a short news report about the assassination of Archduke Franz Ferdinand using the information on these pages and by studying the images, particularly **Source A**.
4. How would the Austro-Hungarian Empire feel about the assassination? What would their reaction be and why?
5. Extend the answers given about Gavrilo Princip by using **Source C** and your own research. What extra details can you fill in? Are any of the details contradictory? What other questions would you ask?
6. **Extension task**: research why the assassination led to the outbreak of the First World War, in preparation for next lesson.

KEY WORDS
assassination
Black Hand gang

FINAL FOCUS
The relationship between the Austrian Empire and Serbia had been strained for a number of years before the assassination. The assassination was a small, but **significant** event in this relationship, because it led to war.

1.3 What caused the First World War?

OBJECTIVES
- Explain the factors that led to the outbreak of the First World War.
- Make a judgement about which causes were long-term and which were short-term.

The events of 28 June 1914 kick-started the First World War. Yet it wasn't just the shooting of Archduke Franz Ferdinand that led to war. Some people might refer to this as simply a **trigger** event. A trigger event is an event that causes a whole host of other events to occur. Before the shooting took place, potential conflicts had been simmering away for a considerable period of time, but it took this event to bring them all to the surface. The assassination was therefore a short-term cause of the war. There were many other causes too – both short- and long-term.

SOURCE A: Can you describe what is happening here? What do you think the point of this cartoon is?

DO YOU WANT TO BE MY FRIEND?

In 1914, two major power **alliances** existed in Europe:

The **Triple Alliance** of Germany, Italy and Austria-Hungary.

The **Triple Entente** of France, Russia and Britain.

These alliances formed because all these nations were rivals for land, trade and political power. They had all agreed to assist each other if any country was aggressive towards them. For example, if France got into trouble, Britain would come to the rescue, and France would return the favour. These alliances were a long-term cause of the war because they had existed for a long period of time.

They had been seen as a way to prevent war: the threat of possible military action was hoped to be enough to keep conflict from occurring. However, once Serbia (where Gavrilo Princip was from) was threatened with war by Austria-Hungary, a chain reaction occurred, bringing the two alliances into the war, as Russia had agreed to support Serbia (see **Source A**).

CAUSES OF THE WAR

These were not the only causes of the war, however. It wasn't quite that simple! The causes can be loosely arranged under the following headings:

- **Militarism** – the desire to have the biggest and best army and navy (see **Source D**).
- **Imperialism** – the desire to have the best collection of countries and to be the richest country.
- **Nationalism** – the desire to be a country that is able to make decisions about what they do and when they do it.

Britain and Germany both wanted superior numbers of 'Dreadnought' battleships.	Franz Ferdinand was assassinated by a Serbian nationalist.
Two major alliances existed – The Triple Entente and the Triple Alliance.	Many European nations wanted to be the most powerful nation.
There was long-standing bitterness between European nations after previous wars.	There was a long history of arguments over territory – such as Alsace Lorraine.

SOURCE B: Causes of the First World War.

4 Britain hadn't yet joined the war, and Germany hoped it would stay that way.

3 After defeating France, Germany's armies would then quickly move troops by rail to take on Russia. They hoped Russia would be slow to mobilize troops.

N

0   60   120 miles
0   90   180 km

GREAT BRITAIN **4**

GERMANY

BELGIUM

1 by rail

3 RUSSIA

•Paris

2 The plan relied on the Germans defeating France quickly – they would make their way through **neutral** countries, such as Belgium, and attack France from the North.

2

FRANCE

1 Germany devised the Schlieffen Plan in 1905 so that they could avoid fighting with both France and Russia at the same time.

SWITZ.

AUSTRIA-HUNGARY

SOURCE C: The **Schlieffen Plan**.

Read the information in **Source C**. In reality, Russia mobilized troops quickly and Germany found far more resistance in Belgium than they had anticipated. On 4 August 1914 Britain declared war on Germany after German forces moved through Belgium. Britain had sworn to protect Belgium, so it went to war in Belgium's defence.

 KEY WORDS

alliance
imperialism
militarism
nationalism
neutral
Schlieffen Plan
trigger

 TASKS

1 Which 'trigger' event led to the outbreak of the First World War?
2 Which nations were in the Triple Alliance and the Triple Entente?
3 Explain the following in your own words:
   a Militarism   **b** Imperialism   **c** Nationalism.
4 Using **Source C**, describe the Schlieffen Plan.
5 Why did the Schlieffen Plan fail?
6 Using **Sources A** and **C**, describe how so many nations became involved in the war.
7 Use the statements shown in **Source B** to explain the causes of the First World War. Do this by:
   a Placing the statements into three columns: Militarism, Nationalism and Imperialism
   b Deciding whether each cause is 'short-' or 'long-' term, and labelling them
   c Using this information to write a short essay detailing the long- and short-term causes of the First World War. You may wish to conduct extra research into this before you begin.

GCSE-STYLE QUESTION

'The First World War began because Germany was aggressive towards Belgium and Britain was defending her interests.' How far do you agree with this statement?

SOURCE D: The launch of the 'Dreadnought' HMS *Collingwood* in 1908.

 FINAL FOCUS

The causes of a conflict are always open to debate and discussion. Often people **change** their points of view **over time**. That is a key aspect of studying history.

1.4 How did the Great War become a global war?

OBJECTIVES
- Identify battlefronts outside Western Europe.
- Explain why countries outside Europe joined in.

SOURCE B: King George V watches American troops on parade in 1918.

A front is the term in war for somewhere fighting takes place. The trenches of the **Western Front** (see Chapter 3) are the most famous battle 'front' in WWI, but there was also action elsewhere in Europe, at sea, in the Middle and Far East; even as far away as Africa.

As the trench war became a **stalemate**, other fronts opened up in the race to beat Germany or her allies. If France and Britain couldn't invade Germany from the west, they hoped they could from the south and east. Countries at war all **mobilized** their troops in their **colonies** to fight each other and help in Europe. All of these factors helped turn the Great War into a global war.

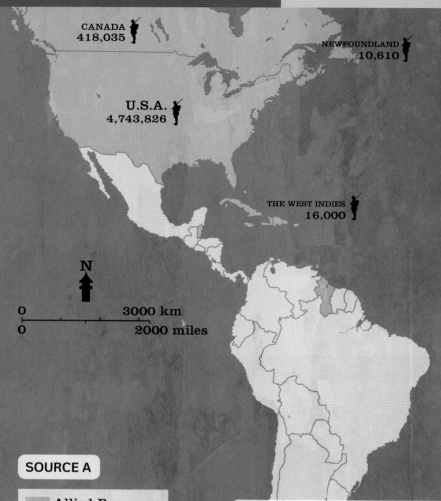

CANADA 418,035
NEWFOUNDLAND 10,610
U.S.A. 4,743,826
THE WEST INDIES 16,000

N

0 3000 km
0 2000 miles

SOURCE A

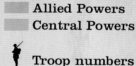

Allied Powers
Central Powers
 Troop numbers

KEY WORDS

- colonies
- mobilize
- stalemate
- Western Front

FINAL FOCUS

The global war was seen by some as a pointless sideshow, by others as a vital course of action that was needed to beat Germany. By 1917, most continents had either seen action or had sent people to fight.

3 The Balkan Campaigns

The Allies were keen to invade Germany through the Turkish (Ottoman) Empire, or get Germany's ally Turkey to surrender. This didn't happen in Europe, with a disastrous troop landing at Gallipoli (see Unit 3.5). However, the British Navy's attack on Turkey's Navy at Constantinople harmed Turkey's war effort. At Salonika in Greece, another Allied invasion attempt ended in stalemate until September 1918. These campaigns caused unhappiness amongst Allied troops and tied up over 1 million Allied soldiers.

GREAT BRITAIN 704,416

GERMANY 11,000,000

BELGIUM 267,000

AUSTRIA-HUNGARY 7,800,000

FRANCE 8,410,000

ROMANIA 750,000

ITALY 5,615,000

BULGARIA 1,200,000

PORTUGAL 65,166

GREECE 230,000

OTTOMAN EMPIRE 2,850,000

RUSSIA 12,000,000

JAPAN 800,000

INDIA 1,524,187

AUSTRALIA 330,000

SOUTH AFRICA 74,196

NEW ZEALAND 100,471

1 The Eastern Front

War on Germany's eastern side was fought by Germany and Austria-Hungary against Russia. It had some trenches, like the Western Front, but it was more a war of movement. At first, war here went well for Russia, despite their soldiers being badly trained and equipped. Many Russians even had to walk to the front! Russia's quick advance, however, meant Germany's Schlieffen Plan failed, leaving Germany surrounded. As war continued, Russia suffered hardship. Russia dropped out of the war, leading Germany to launch one last big offensive against the West, which failed, and Germany surrendered.

2 The Italian Front

Italy agreed to fight alongside Germany before WWI, but in 1915 Italy changed sides to fight against Austria-Hungary for land. This led to Austria having to fight two enemies on two fronts. Austria surrendered by November 1918, leaving Germany with the choice to surrender or fight its enemies on its own.

4 The Middle East

Another offensive against Turkey from 1916 in what's now Iraq and into Palestine used over 1 million British, Australian, New Zealand and Indian troops as well as Arabs under the control of the legendary T.E. Lawrence (Lawrence of Arabia). Advances made against the Turks led to their surrender in November 1918, helping to force Germany to surrender.

5 The War in Africa

By 1916 Britain had captured many of Germany's African colonies, with the help of South Africa. This was at a cost of 130,000 soldiers being kept busy that could have otherwise fought on the Western Front.

 TASKS

1 Using **Source A**, make a list of the places where fighting took place outside of Western Europe in the First World War.

2 Make a table like the one below and complete it using the information on these pages.

Battlefront	No. on map	Countries involved	Aim of the campaign

3 Using your table and the information on these pages, answer the following questions.
  a Why did European countries fighting in Europe encourage the war to spread elsewhere?
  b Why did other countries outside of Europe get involved?

GCSE-STYLE QUESTION

How far do you agree that the Great War deserves the name 'World War I'? Use your knowledge and the information on these pages.

2.1 Joining up

OBJECTIVES
- Suggest reasons why people joined the British Army.
- Explain why some people had to be conscripted into the army.
- Analyse sources to find out how people felt about joining up.

KEY WORDS

BEF
conscription
navy
recruitment
trenches
volunteer

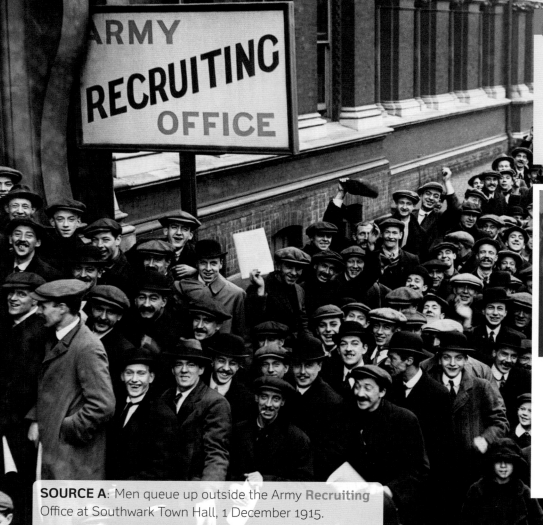

SOURCE A: Men queue up outside the Army **Recruiting** Office at Southwark Town Hall, 1 December 1915.

SOURCE B: Men not fit enough for the war were offered free physical training at the YMCA. This photo is from a film advertising this training. How reliable is this photo, and **Source A**, for history students? Why?

Not many people today can say that they have experienced the feelings connected with knowing that you will be leaving home and going to war. Modern charities such as 'Help for Heroes' acknowledge the true nature of the sacrifice that is being made. Those who go into war put their lives on the line. How would you feel if you were faced with a decision like this?

VOLUNTEERS

In 1914, Britain had only a small army because it relied mainly on its **navy** for protection. Part of the army was a specially trained unit of 120,000 men, known as the **British Expeditionary Force** (BEF). As the reality of the fighting became apparent, the BEF losses began to increase. The call for **volunteers** to join up was met with huge enthusiasm. It was hoped that 100,000 men would answer the call, but by the end of 1915, nearly 2.5 million men had volunteered.

Many men who joined up were expecting the war to be over by Christmas, which meant that they were not anticipating a long-term commitment. There was a positive feeling in the air. New soldiers were marched off in street parades, and flowers were thrown at the new recruits. They were given cigarettes and chocolates by the onlookers.

CONSCRIPTION

By 1915, thousands of men had been killed. Volunteer numbers fell as the truth about the war in France emerged. There was not going to be a quick victory, and the conditions in many of the **trenches** were appalling. 3.4 million eligible men in Britain had not volunteered, and this concerned the government.

Conscription was introduced in January 1916, allowing the government to 'call up' any single men aged between 18 and 41. In May, this was extended to married men. By April 1918, an extra 2.5 million soldiers had joined the army.

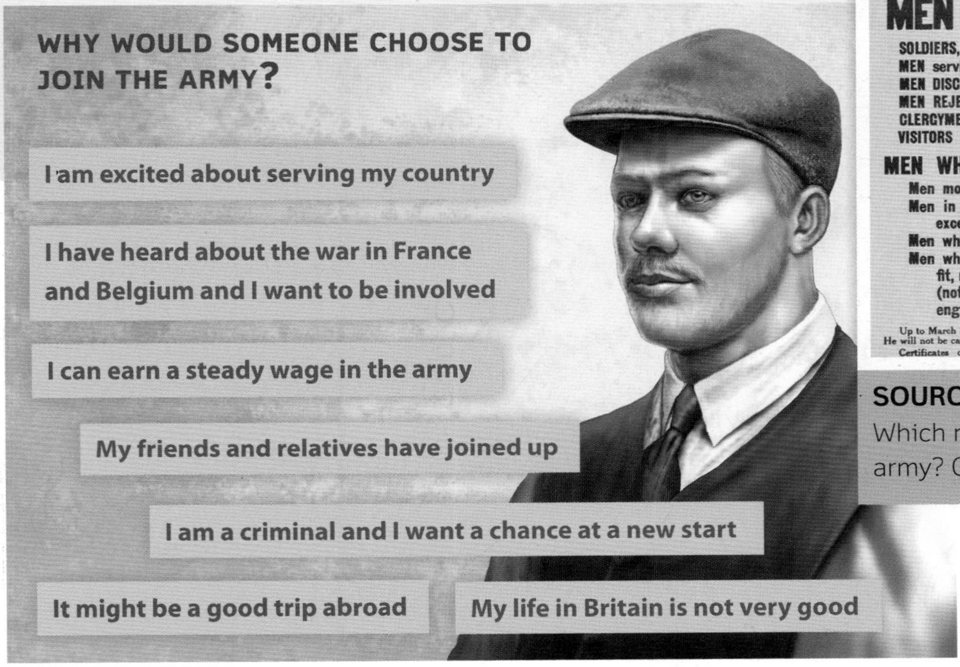

WHY WOULD SOMEONE CHOOSE TO JOIN THE ARMY?

I am excited about serving my country

I have heard about the war in France and Belgium and I want to be involved

I can earn a steady wage in the army

My friends and relatives have joined up

I am a criminal and I want a chance at a new start

It might be a good trip abroad

My life in Britain is not very good

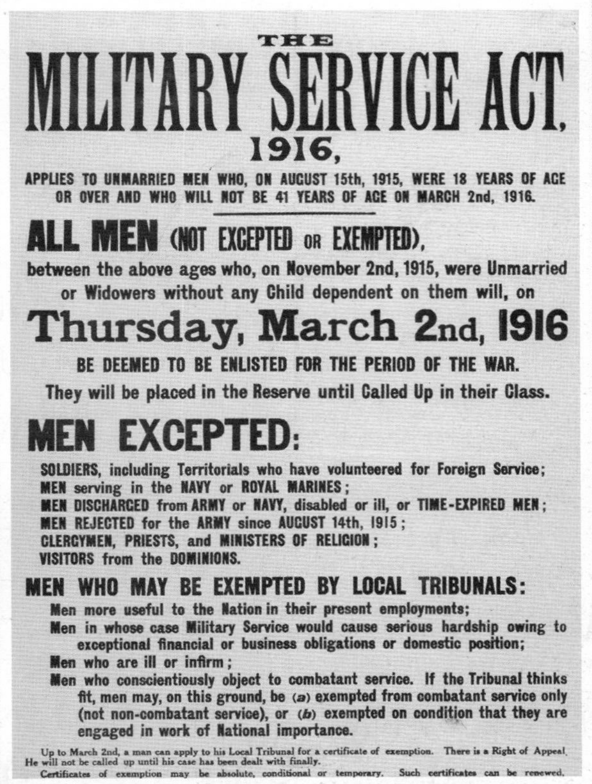

THE MILITARY SERVICE ACT, 1916,

APPLIES TO UNMARRIED MEN WHO, ON AUGUST 15th, 1915, WERE 18 YEARS OF AGE OR OVER AND WHO WILL NOT BE 41 YEARS OF AGE ON MARCH 2nd, 1916.

ALL MEN (NOT EXCEPTED OR EXEMPTED),

between the above ages who, on November 2nd, 1915, were Unmarried or Widowers without any Child dependent on them will, on

Thursday, March 2nd, 1916

BE DEEMED TO BE ENLISTED FOR THE PERIOD OF THE WAR.

They will be placed in the Reserve until Called Up in their Class.

MEN EXCEPTED:

SOLDIERS, including Territorials who have volunteered for Foreign Service;
MEN serving in the NAVY or ROYAL MARINES;
MEN DISCHARGED from ARMY or NAVY, disabled or ill, or TIME-EXPIRED MEN;
MEN REJECTED for the ARMY since AUGUST 14th, 1915;
CLERGYMEN, PRIESTS, and MINISTERS OF RELIGION;
VISITORS from the DOMINIONS.

MEN WHO MAY BE EXEMPTED BY LOCAL TRIBUNALS:

Men more useful to the Nation in their present employments;
Men in whose case Military Service would cause serious hardship owing to exceptional financial or business obligations or domestic position;
Men who are ill or infirm;
Men who conscientiously object to combatant service. If the Tribunal thinks fit, men may, on this ground, be (*a*) exempted from combatant service only (not non-combatant service), or (*b*) exempted on condition that they are engaged in work of National importance.

Up to March 2nd, a man can apply to his Local Tribunal for a certificate of exemption. There is a Right of Appeal. He will not be called up until his case has been dealt with finally.
Certificates of exemption may be absolute, conditional or temporary. Such certificates can be renewed.

SOURCE C: The Military Service Act of 1916. Which men were not expected to serve in the army? Can you suggest why?

The army's stature had suffered during the Boer War, when after repeated debacles [failures], its efficiency came to be fundamentally questioned… The reaction of one mother to her eighteen-year-old's enlistment [joining up] was typical of many. 'Oh', she said, 'you little fool, don't you understand there's only thieves and vagabonds [strays] join the army, you go back and tell them that you've changed your mind.'

SOURCE D: The historian Richard Van Emden, writing in *Boy Soldiers of the Great War.*

✓ TASKS

1. a What was the BEF?
    b How many men were originally in this force?
    c How many men did they hope would join up?
    d How many men had joined up by the end of 1915?
2. Look at the 'thoughts' surrounding the British man on this page. Put them in order ranked from 1 to 7, where 1 is the 'most likely reason' and 7 is the 'least likely reason' he might have for joining up.
3. Read **Source D**.
    a What did the boy's mother say about the army?
    b What other information does the source give us about the army?
4. In a format of your choice, explain why men joined up to fight in the First World War. Include the key words 'volunteer', 'recruitment' and 'conscription'.
5. Imagine that you have just heard the announcement of war. Using what you have learned in this lesson, explain why you *would* or *would not* volunteer to fight.

◉ FINAL FOCUS

What is army recruitment like today? Does conscription exist?

2.2 Recruiting the troops

OBJECTIVES
- Describe the messages that **recruitment** posters contained.
- Explain why recruitment posters were used.
- Make a judgement about which posters were most effective and why.

SOURCE A: A Major inspects new recruits in the First World War.

In today's world we are surrounded by advertising. It comes into our homes via the television, radio and Internet. We can easily watch or read the news on a daily basis to catch up on events. Other people can influence our views instantly through the power of advertising. Advertising existed in the era of the Great War, but how people were exposed to it was very different. The initial news of the war would have come through printed media – newspapers and posters, for example.

JOINING UP

Many men joined up to fight in 1914 and 1915 without having to be forced or heavily persuaded. They were doing it to fight for their King and country and to protect their loved ones. They were largely unaware, or naïve, about the dangers of war. They hadn't experienced loss of loved ones, or the psychological trauma of a modern war. Once the initial enthusiasm for war began to dry up and people realized what war really involved, the government had to 'persuade' people to join the army. They had two main ways of doing this:

- Powerful **propaganda** (the use of media to influence a person's point of view) and recruitment posters.
- **Conscription** (making it compulsory to join up).

 PEOPLE OF WWI: LORD KITCHENER

One of the most famous faces from the First World War is Lord Kitchener, the Secretary of State for War. His face was on the recruitment poster which inspired many men to join up. Kitchener died in 1916 when the boat that he was travelling on was sunk by a torpedo.

SOURCE B

KEY WORDS

conscription
propaganda
recruitment

WHAT MAKES AN EFFECTIVE RECRUITMENT POSTER?

Great time and money was spent designing the posters that would be used to persuade or inspire men and women to join the war effort. This was especially important once the initial flood of troops had subsided. The government wanted to convey certain messages which would make people want to risk their own lives.

SOURCE C

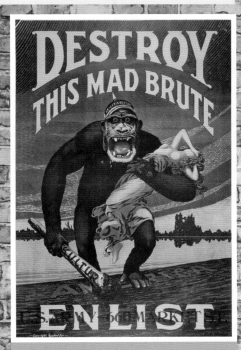

SOURCE D

Daddy, what did _YOU_ do in the Great War?

SOURCE E

FINAL FOCUS

Propaganda is still used today in many forms. How do you know that what you are reading in the media or seeing on your screens is not focused upon making you think or act in a certain way? A good example is modern television advertising. Are you falling for its hidden messages?

A desire to see the world   PATRIOTISM   HEROISM

Positivity   **Assurance of victory**   GUILT   Shame

A love of the Empire   **PRIDE**

Appeals to a personal ideal or motive   Sense of adventure

Fear of German culture   A desire to fight

✓ TASKS

1. Why did many people initially want to fight in the war?
2. What is propaganda?
3. Why did the government need to use posters to recruit troops?
4. Look at **Sources B** to **E**. Explain what message each poster is trying to put across.
5. Look at the box of words and phrases on this page and decide which posters each one relates to. You must make a decision about which are the most relevant to each poster – remember, this is your opinion and you must explain your choices.
6. Compare two of the posters and explain their similarities and differences and why you think each one was designed in that way. Which is the most effective and why?
7. Germany also used propaganda to persuade people to join the war effort. How would their posters have been similar or different to the British ones?
8. Create your own recruitment poster, using the important words and examples given on these pages to help you.

2.3 Pals Battalions

OBJECTIVES
- Explain what a **Pals Battalion** is.
- Suggest why men joined up to fight in these battalions.
- Judge whether Pals Battalions were a good or bad idea.

SOURCE A: Men from a Hull Pals Battalion marching near Doullens, 28 June 1916.

STOP THE CLOCK

28 August 1914 – Lord Derby established the first Pals Battalion in Liverpool.

Doing something new can mean that you feel afraid of what's ahead of you. Going to a new school for the first day, for example, or having a doctors' appointment, might be daunting. To get over these feelings, many people would take somebody with them. Would you?

Many young men felt the same about joining the army. They felt compelled to join up, but going with somebody they knew would make the experience easier – so they joined up with friends, work colleagues and family members.

THE SUCCESS OF PALS BATTALIONS

One of the reasons why recruitment to the British armies was so successful initially was because of the 'Pals' (or 'Chums') Battalions. The idea of these battalions was to persuade men to join up with their friends and work colleagues, so that they could serve together. Perhaps they were all hoping that the war would be friendly and full of companionship, as well as a mental and physical challenge. This idea proved to be incredibly popular. Alongside men joining up to serve and protect their country, the government had now got the added bonus of men joining up to have fun!

Some of the battalions that were formed included Tyneside Irish, Footballers' Battalion, Stockbrokers' Battalion, Judeans, Glasgow Tramways' Battalion, Post Office Rifles, Accrington Pals, Leeds Pals, Bantams (for men below the minimum height) and Liverpool Dockers Battalion.

PEOPLE OF WWI

A member of the Footballers' Battalion was Captain Vivian Woodward. As well as being a Captain in the British Army he had been one of a number of professional footballers who served in the war. Woodward served on the Somme, having also captained England, Spurs and Chelsea before the war.

SOURCE B: Captain Vivian Woodward.

KEY WORDS

incentive
Pals Battalion
trauma

SOURCE C: Liverpool Dockers Battalion march through Liverpool while watched by the public.

WHAT WERE THE PROS AND CONS OF PALS BATTALIONS?

SOURCE E

A real **incentive** to join the army.

A massive social loss for the areas that the soldiers came from.

Large numbers of men were called up quickly.

Recruits were positive and in good spirits.

Whole villages and groups of young men were wiped out, sometimes in one day.

Workplaces suffered.

Areas never recovered from the trauma.

Towns and villages helped out with the recruitment drive.

THE DISADVANTAGES

However powerful the Pals Battalion scheme may have been, a terrible disadvantage of it was that its men, as well as training together, also fought and often died together. If they came from the same community, it meant that whole villages and towns could lose a large proportion of their young men. For example, the Battle of the Somme in 1916 saw the death of 750 of the 900 Leeds Pals, and 584 of the 720 Accrington Pals. The **trauma** of small communities losing hundreds of sons, husbands and fathers was a terrible feature of the war. The sheer scale of the casualties within the Leeds and Accrington Pals means that the tale of the Pals Battalions will always be told as one of great sorrow – but this is not the entire story (see **Source E**).

In Accrington, recruitment began on 14 September, with 104 men accepted for service in the first three hours. Brothers, cousins, friends and workmates enlisted together and within ten days the Accrington Pals had reached full strength of some 1000 men.

SOURCE D: Written by historian and journalist Bruce Robinson, www.bbc.co.uk.

 FINAL FOCUS

Although there were great losses in the Accrington and Leeds Pals, such losses were not common. Why do you think such tragedies are mentioned again and again?

 TASKS

1 a When was the first Pals Battalion set up and who was it set up by?
  b Name two Pals Battalions.
2 Read **Source D**.
  a Which battalion is mentioned in the source?
  b How many men would have to join a Pals Battalion for it to be at full strength?
  c Is **Source D** useful for informing us about Pals Battalions? Is it a reliable source of information?
3 What happened to the Accrington and Leeds Pals at the Battle of the Somme?
4 Look at the statements about the Pals Battalions in **Source E**. Put the statements into two columns under the headings 'Pros' and 'Cons'. Then write two paragraphs summarizing the points and adding your own if possible.
5 Make a judgement: were Pals Battalions a good or a bad idea? Why?
6 Research one of the other Pals Battalions mentioned on these pages. Can you present your teacher with the information that you have found out by next lesson?

GCSE-STYLE QUESTION
What was the significance of Pals Battalions?

2.4 Empire and Commonwealth troops

OBJECTIVES
- Describe the role of the **British Empire** in supplying troops for the First World War.
- Judge how significant these men were.

SOURCE A: Commonwealth troops march past on parade in Marseilles, France, during the First World War.

SOURCE B: From the British Government website.

During the First World War, 1.2 million soldiers from undivided India served with the Allies, 74,000 of whom made the ultimate sacrifice. Baroness Warsi, whose grandfathers fought in the Second World War, said: 'As I have said before, our boys weren't just Tommies; they were Tariqs and Tajinders too'.

When people talk about 'British soldiers', what do you think they mean? What is 'British'? At the start of the First World War, many more people than today could claim to be British, because of the British Empire and **Commonwealth**. The British Empire was a collection of countries that came under British rule. At its height, the British Empire was the biggest empire that has ever existed. During the First World War, Britain's Empire reached across the globe, including India, Australia, New Zealand, Canada, the Caribbean and parts of Africa. Although the inhabitants of these countries were not living in Britain, they still joined the fight for Britain and its allies.

SOLDIERS FROM AUSTRALIA AND NEW ZEALAND

The ANZACs (Australian and New Zealand Army Corps) were formed from excellent soldiers and were well received by the British. Australia offered 330,000 troops to the war effort. Australia also tried on two occasions to introduce conscription, but it was twice voted against – in 1916 and 1917. The ANZACs served bravely at Gallipoli and on the Western Front.

SOLDIERS FROM THE CARIBBEAN

'West Indian' soldiers saw action on many battlefronts, most notably the Middle East, France and Italy. Some were pilots in the newly formed Royal Flying Corps.

KEY WORDS

British Empire
Commonwealth
Victoria Cross

STOP THE CLOCK

26 September 1914 – troops from the British Empire began to arrive on the Western Front to fight for Britain.

CASE STUDY: SOLDIERS FROM INDIA

More than 1.5 million Indian citizens fought for Britain and its allies, serving in the Royal Flying Corps and in the army, and nearly 65,000 died. Why would these citizens have left their homes to fight in a war thousands of miles away? These extracts give some of the possible reasons – see if you can identify them.

It is quite impossible that I should return alive. [But] don't be grieved at my death, because I shall die arms in hand, wearing the warrior's clothes. This is the most happy death that anyone can die.

SOURCE C: A letter from Indar Singh, a soldier fighting in the Battle of the Somme, 1916.

...our father the King-Emperor of India [George V] needs us, and any of us who refuses to help him in his need should be counted among the most polluted sinners. It is our first duty to show loyal gratitude to Government.

SOURCE D: A letter from a wounded Sikh in England, January 1915.

'The British authorities considered introducing conscription, but instead adopted a 'quota' system. From 1916, Indian officials were told to produce a given number of men from a particular district, or face losing their jobs. The officials used bribery and even coercion to find the necessary recruits, leading to some discontent in the main recruiting grounds.'

SOURCE E: Written by historian David Omissi, 2011.

He who dies on the field of battle,
His name never dies, but lives in history

SOURCE F: An extract from a poem sent home by Dafadar Nathan Singh, France, April 1916.

 PEOPLE OF WWI

Many Empire soldiers fought bravely for Britain and were awarded the **Victoria Cross**. During the German attack on Hollebeke near Belgium, Khan was part of the Indian Baluch regiment (known as Baluchis). Many of them were killed or wounded.

SOURCE G: Khudadad Khan.

Two of the Baluchi machine gun crews carried on fighting. One was destroyed with a direct hit. The other was overrun by Germans and everyone was bayoneted or shot, Khudadad Khan amongst them. He was the only one to survive. He pretended to be dead. When night came he crawled away and rejoined what was left of his regiment. For his remarkable courage, Khudadad Khan was the first Indian soldier to be awarded the Victoria Cross.

SOURCE H: An account of Khudadad Khan's bravery.

TASKS

1. a What was the 'British Empire'? Name two of its countries.
    b What does ANZAC stand for?
2. Read **Source B**.
    a How does the figure stated for the number of Indian soldiers serving in the First World War differ from the information given on this page? Why do you think this is?
    b What does **Source B** tell us about the names of some of the Indian soldiers who served in the First World War?
3. Using **Sources C** to **F**, explain why Indian soldiers fought in the war.
4. Write a short news report about Khudadad Khan in Hollebeke.
5. **Extension task**: Research the experiences of Indian soldiers during the war. Why did many of them have positive experiences? And how bad did it get for others?

FINAL FOCUS

People today often don't realize that Commonwealth troops fought for Britain. Why do you think this is?

2.5 Boy soldiers

OBJECTIVES
- Describe what is meant by the term 'boy soldier'.
- Explain why young boys were able to join the army.

Some things seem like a really good idea when you are young. Have you ever been in a situation where you have been desperate to do something but people around you have been telling you not to? What about going to war? How would a child feel about that?

KEY WORDS

prospect
requirements
restrictions
underage

PEOPLE OF WWI

John Travers Cornwell (see **Source A**) was one of the youngest boys to win the Victoria Cross for his heroic actions at the Battle of Jutland. He stayed at his post on HMS *Chester* while all around him were dying. Cornwell died of his wounds on 2 June 1916, aged 16.

SOURCE A: John Travers Cornwell was fatally wounded at the age of 16. Here, sailors pay their respects.

BOYS JOIN UP

Some young boys wanted to go to war. What is surprising is that any young boys were recruited at all, given that initially recruits had to be between 18 and 30 years old, at least 1.6m tall, and have a chest measurement of no less than 863mm. It was because these **requirements** were not stuck to rigidly that some boys as young as 13 were able to join up. Birth certificates were rarely inspected (and many men did not have one anyway), and recruiting officers relied on their own judgement as to whether candidates were mature enough. Minimum height **restrictions** were also relaxed in some places, to enable more men to join up when there was a lull in numbers volunteering.

Why might boys want to join up?	Why did the army accept them?
• A relative had been killed	• They had lied about their age
• They were bored	• They had given a false name
• They had to do long hours at work or school	• There weren't enough recruits
• Schooling was only compulsory until age 14	• Physical characteristics were more important than age
• There were no jobs	• Recruiting sergeants were paid per recruit
• It was an exciting **prospect**	• Their parents had no issue with it
• Their friends were joining up	• They were needed to help win the war
• They did not want to live with their parents	
• They liked being outdoors	
• They wanted to see an end to the war	

SOURCE B

21 Park Avenue, Dublin

Dear Lord Kitchener

I am an Irish boy 9 years of age and I want to go to the front. I can ride jolly quick on my bicycle and would go as a dispatch ridder. I wouldn't let the germans get it. I am a good shot with a revolver and would kill a good few of the Germans. I am very strong and often win a fight with lads twice as big as myself. I want a uneform and a revolver and will give a good account of myself. Please send an ancner

Yours affectionately

Alfie Knight

SOURCE C: A letter written by Alfie Knight to Lord Kitchener.

The child, said to be too short to see over the edge of a trench was recalled by another **underage** soldier, George Maher, who was only 13 when he was sent to the Somme during the First World War. Mr Maher, who died aged 96 in 1999, remembered, 'I was locked up in a train under guard, one of five underage boys caught serving on the front being sent back to England. The youngest was twelve years old. A little nugget bloke he was too. We joked that the other soldiers would have had to have lifted him up to see over the trenches.'

SOURCE D: An extract from an article written by Julie Henry – a journalist for the *Daily Telegraph* – quoting George Maher, a First World War 'boy soldier'.

On 24th October 1913, nearly a year before the outbreak of war, he turned up at an army recruitment office in the city. Captain J.P.T. Mackesy, JP, witnessed the paperwork, as John joined up for six years' service with the 3rd Battalion, Royal Irish Regiment, Army Reserve. On 25th October he stood in front of a medical officer who gave him the regulation physical examination. The records show he was 5 feet 3 inches tall and weighed less than 8 ½ stone [1.6m and 54kg].

Some ten years later a farmer tilling his field unearthed his remains. They were taken to a cemetery at Poelcapelle, where he was buried in Plot 6, Row F, Grave 1.

SOURCE E: An extract from a book by Neil Oliver – a historian and television presenter – about the 'boy soldier' John Condon.

 FINAL FOCUS

Even by the standards of 1914 to 1918, some of the boys who joined up to fight were very young and could barely have passed as adults. Today, these boys would perhaps appear even younger, given that they would have had a generally poorer diet and healthcare. Was it really acceptable for any of these boy soldiers to be at war? Who should have taken the blame for their being killed or injured in conflict?

 TASKS

1 a   How old were soldiers required to be?
   b   How tall?
   c   What chest size?
2 Give two reasons why many boy soldiers were accepted into the army.
3 Read **Source C**.
   a   Why does this boy think that he would be a good soldier?
   b   What do you notice about the language he uses?
   c   Rewrite the source in a grammatically correct form, making appropriate changes to the spelling and punctuation.

4 Read **Source D**.
   a   What is unusual about the boy mentioned in the source?
   b   Would George Maher have been a reliable witness?
5 Read **Source E**. What happened to John Condon? Why is he unusual as a soldier?
6 Use the information in **Source B** to explain why boys joined up and why they were accepted.

2.6 Choosing not to fight

OBJECTIVES
- Explain why some people decided not to fight.
- Make a judgement about whether you would have fought.

SOURCE A: Angry crowds surround and attack a London church where pacifists are meeting during the First World War.

KEY WORDS

absolutist
alternativist
conscience
conscientious objector
pacifist
White Feather Campaign

Have you ever been in a situation where you've felt different from those around you? Have you ever made a decision that you know will make you unpopular? During the First World War, there were people who went against the grain and decided not to fight. Why do you think this is?

CONSCIENTIOUS OBJECTORS

Someone who says they won't fight in a war is called a **conscientious objector** (CO), also known as 'conchies'. These people had different reasons for not fighting, most often because their **consciences** did not allow them to. They may have been **pacifists** who believed in peace, such as Quakers, or people who simply objected to others taking away their freedom. It is estimated that there were about 20,000 COs in total in the First World War. It's important to understand that not all COs chose not to go to war; they simply chose not to fight. Some of these men took on non-fighting roles in the army, such as ambulance drivers or cooks. They worked on the front lines alongside troops.

SOURCE B: Why might someone object to going to war?

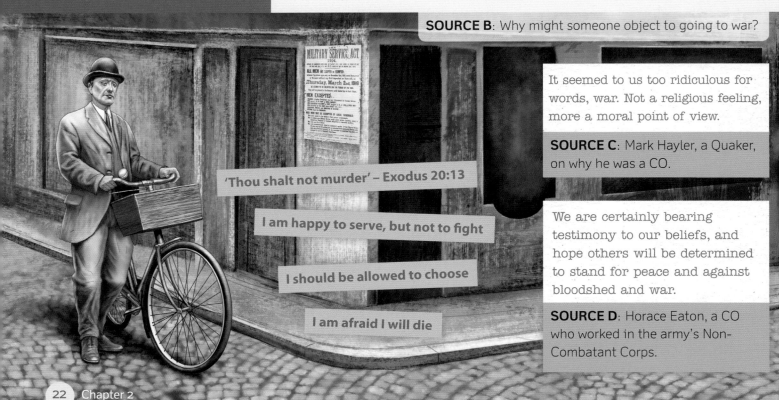

'Thou shalt not murder' – Exodus 20:13

I am happy to serve, but not to fight

I should be allowed to choose

I am afraid I will die

It seemed to us too ridiculous for words, war. Not a religious feeling, more a moral point of view.

SOURCE C: Mark Hayler, a Quaker, on why he was a CO.

We are certainly bearing testimony to our beliefs, and hope others will be determined to stand for peace and against bloodshed and war.

SOURCE D: Horace Eaton, a CO who worked in the army's Non-Combatant Corps.

ALTERNATIVISTS AND ABSOLUTISTS

Other men helped the war effort without joining the army. They took on civilian roles and were called **alternativists**. A relatively small number of men (about 1000) refused to contribute at all to the war effort. They believed the war was wrong and were called **absolutists**.

THE TREATMENT OF 'CONCHIES'

COs were often labelled as cowards by members of the public. The **White Feather Campaign** was set up to humiliate men into joining up. Women patrolled the streets, handing out white feathers (a symbol of cowardice) to men who were not in uniform.

All COs had to face tribunals (interview panels with a legal authority) that checked whether or not the men had genuine moral objections to joining up. These tribunals were run by local councils and often included older businessmen, landowners and retired military men. There was always one military person present, whose main aim was to recruit as many men as possible for the army. The COs did not always get a sympathetic hearing, and relatively few succeeded. Those who refused to join up could be sent to prison, and almost 6000 were.

COs who ended up in prison were often treated harshly. Over 70 died in prison, as a result of illness or suicide, and many suffered long-term physical or mental illness. At the end of the war in November 1918 there was a delay in releasing many of the COs from prison. Some remained there for another six months. Even on their release, they found that many people refused to employ them, and signs such as 'COs and absolutists need not apply' appeared in some job adverts.

SOURCE E: A propaganda postcard issued in 1915. The image refers to a line from a nursery rhyme.

" THIS   LITTLE   PIG   STAYED   AT   HOME "

 PEOPLE OF WWI

In 1918, after four years in the trenches, brothers John and Arthur Hunter became conscientious objectors. They were publicly humiliated, stripped of the right to vote and their parents never spoke to them again.

SOURCE F: Taken from the article 'The brothers who made a stand' by Sabine Durrant, www.guardian.com. Why do you think the brothers were 'stripped of the right to vote'? Is this source for or against COs?

✓ **TASKS**

1 a What is a conscientious objector?
   b Write definitions for these terms: pacifist, alternativist, absolutist.
   c How many conscientious objectors were there during the war?
   d What did some men choose to do instead of fighting?
2 Look at **Sources B** to **D**.
   a What reasons have been given for not wanting to fight?
   b Which of the reasons is not one of 'conscience'?
3 Explain what the White Feather Campaign was.
4 Look at **Source E**.
   a Who is the person on the left supposed to represent?
   b Write a paragraph explaining the intended message of this source. Refer to: the poster, what the men are wearing, the nursery rhyme.
   c How useful is this source for showing us how people felt about COs?

GCSE-STYLE QUESTION
'Conscientious objectors were cowards.' How far do you agree with this point of view?

 FINAL FOCUS

Would you have fought? Explain why in no fewer than 200 words.

3.1 What were the trenches like?

OBJECTIVES
- Explain what a **trench** is.
- Describe the layout of a trench.
- Explain why trenches were built in this way and for what purpose.

A trench is a hole in the ground that is approximately 2 metres deep. It is used to keep soldiers, supplies and artillery safe and out of sight of the enemy. The opposing armies dug themselves into trenches: the Germans on one side, the British and French on the other. Over the next four years, each side launched attacks to break through enemy lines.

The trenches ran for a huge length across Europe from the North Sea to Switzerland. Such an expanse of trench systems inevitably meant a huge variety of conditions. The popular image you might have already seen of trenches with mud, rats, and endless puddles may have been true in certain parts of the line, but not in all. There was a large difference in the quality of trenches between the countries, and between wetter and dryer parts of British/French trenches. The Germans had excellent trench systems, much better and deeper than many others.

SOURCE A: The main purpose of a trench was the protection of the soldiers. What protective features can you see?

Sandbags

Entrance to a tunnel

Tommy

Trench mortar

Corned beef

Rats

Water

Mud

SOURCE C: An impressively built German trench on the Western Front in February 1917.

SOURCE B: A trench mortar.

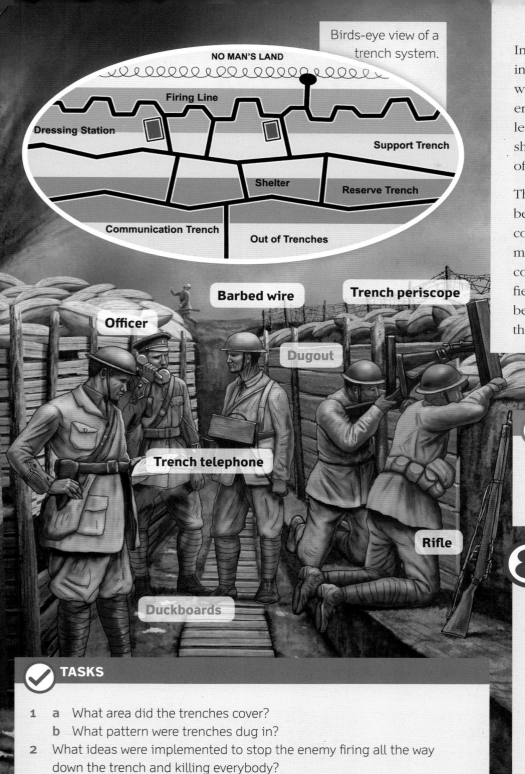

Birds-eye view of a trench system.

NO MAN'S LAND

Firing Line

Dressing Station

Support Trench

Shelter

Reserve Trench

Communication Trench

Out of Trenches

Barbed wire

Trench periscope

Officer

Dugout

Trench telephone

Rifle

Duckboards

Individual trenches were named and included a series of **fire bays** and walkways that were designed to stop enemy troops firing down the whole length of the trench, and prevent shell blasts devastating whole lines of exposed trench.

The lines of trenches had to be kitted out with appropriate communications. As well as messages sent by runners, communication was mainly by field telephone, so cables had to be laid both within and between the trenches.

KEY WORDS

duckboard
dugout
fire bay
trench

PEOPLE OF WWI

Francis Phillip Woodruff (aka Frank Richards) wrote a book about life in the trenches, from the perspective of a low-ranking soldier. The book was called *Old Soldiers Never Die*. Would the diary of an ordinary soldier be useful to people studying the trenches? Would it be more or less useful than that of an officer? Why?

FINAL FOCUS

The design and layout of the trenches made all the difference in the outcome of battles on the front. What do you think the best trenches would have been like?

TASKS

1 a What area did the trenches cover?
   b What pattern were trenches dug in?
2 What ideas were implemented to stop the enemy firing all the way down the trench and killing everybody?
3 Using the image on these pages, sketch your own diagram of a trench. On your diagram:
   a Label the key features of the trench.
   b Next to each label, try to explain what the feature is for, using the text on the spread and your own research.
   c Add to your diagram any more information and details that you can find out.
4 You are a soldier in the trenches on the Western Front. Write a diary entry on your first day. What are the trenches like? How do you feel?

3.2 What was it like to serve in the trenches?

OBJECTIVES
- Explain what day-to-day life was like in a trench.
- Evaluate the dangers of trench life.

Life in the trenches was largely boring. Aside from pre-planned **trench raids**, when small groups of men crept out to check enemy positions or capture prisoners, the only real activity was the **stand to** every morning. This was when soldiers manned the **fire step** of the trench and were alert in case of an enemy attack. For the rest of the time, they were occupied with repairs to trenches, bringing up supplies, or trying to stay warm, dry and fed.

KEY WORDS

fire step
latrines
lice
rations
stand to
trench foot
trench raids

STOP THE CLOCK

The Battle of Mons – the first big battle of the war – took place on 23 August 1914 and was one of the only battles that did not rely on trenches as the main defence for troops.

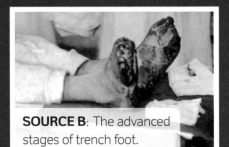

SOURCE B: The advanced stages of trench foot.

SOURCE A: British soldiers take a break as they dig a new trench in an unknown location.

THE SMELL OF ATTACK

The worst conditions facing the soldiers were during actual trench attacks and battles. Shells of all sizes whistled overhead and machine-gun bullets pinged off the trench walls. The strong smell of cordite – an explosive powder – wafted across the battlefield as shells exploded. Some men managed to conquer their fears better than others during these attacks, but for all of them the possibility of violent and sudden death was never far away. Fighting amidst the smell of death was made even worse by the smell of gas, sweat and excrement.

LICE

The water supply was limited, so washing facilities were poor. Most soldiers wore the same clothes for days, and therefore became riddled with **lice**. These blood suckers, no bigger than a grain of rice, caused intense itching.

TRENCH FOOT

Soldiers sometimes suffered from **trench foot**, which was a bit like getting frost bite on their feet. It was caused by having to stand in soaking wet boots for hours at a time. The only cure was changing socks as often as possible (when supplies allowed), and making sure regular foot inspections were carried out. One idea of rubbing whale grease into feet to keep out the wet actually turned out to make it even worse!

FOOD

Food was particularly hard to stomach. The main food on offer was bread, so-called 'Bully' beef (corned beef), and Maconochie, which was a meat-and-vegetable stew in a tin. Soldiers drank water and a daily rum **ration**. In comparison, however, food was even worse for German soldiers, and even in some locations on the Home Front.

LATRINES

Toilets in the trenches were known as **latrines**, and they definitely weren't private (see **Source C**).

> The latrine arrangements were pretty primitive... the army set aside an area of grass field at the edge of the village where the pioneer or sanitary men dug a dozen little trenches, three feet long by one foot wide [90 × 30cm] and about three feet deep [90cm], and without any canvas sacking or anything to hide the view, one dropped one's trousers, bestrode a trench, crouched and attended to nature.

SOURCE C: A description of a trench latrine by historian Neil Hanson.

 FINAL FOCUS

Some historians would say it's tempting for History students to imagine that every soldier had to face unpleasant conditions, but that's not a balanced view. Why might it be tempting to think like this?

UNIFORM

Shrapnel helmet

Tunic

Shirt

Great coat

Trousers

Putees

Rifle

Boots

SOURCE D

 TASKS

1 a What was life in the trenches generally like?
   b What did the soldiers spend time doing?
   c When did the worst conditions in the trenches occur?
2 Read the information about the problems that the soldiers would face in the trenches. Write a short paragraph to describe these problems.
3 In your opinion, which problem was the worst for the soldiers to face and why?
4 Read **Source C**. What was it like to use a latrine in the First World War? How do you know?
5 Look at **Source D**.
   a Describe the clothing and equipment the soldier is expected to wear.

   b Do you think this uniform will protect him against the challenges he will face? Why or why not?
6 You are writing a letter home from the trenches to your parents. Normally the censor would edit out all the details that would make life seem bad. On this occasion the letter has got through. Include as many challenging aspects of trench life as you can. Your teacher will be able to tell you even more.

GCSE-STYLE QUESTION

'Life in the trenches was dull rather than dangerous.' Using the sources on pages 24–27 and your own knowledge, explain whether you agree.

3.3 What was it like to 'go over the top'?

OBJECTIVES
- Explain what is meant by 'going over the top'.
- Analyse stories from soldiers who went over the top.

SOURCE A: Soldiers climb out of their trench and head towards the enemy.

Most people never face real **fear**. They may feel sick when queuing up for a rollercoaster, or have nerves before an exam, but deep down they know that these are safe activities. There were certain times during the First World War when soldiers faced a very real fear of death. After certain attacks, being alive at the end was just down to good luck.

NO MAN'S LAND

The most common form of attack from the trenches was when large numbers of soldiers climbed out of their own trench, tried to cross the open land ahead and then attempted to capture the enemy's trench. This was called 'going over the top' and was one of the most terrifying parts of trench warfare.

No Man's Land – the area lying between the trench lines – was usually filled with barbed wire, shell holes, mud, parts of bodies and rusting bits of army equipment. Anyone crossing it was exposed to enemy fire and their chances of survival were slim.

 PEOPLE OF WWI: ARTHUR BARRACLOUGH

I always said a prayer before going over the top ... I'll never forget it. 'Dear God, I am going into grave danger. Please help me to act like a man and come back safe.' And that's what I did. And I went over without **fear**. That little prayer seemed to save my life because I had no fear left, although there were shells and bullets and all the rest flying when we went over... It's real funny that that prayer put me where I am now... And six times I went up and six times I said that little prayer and each time I went up and come back safe. And I thank God for it every time.

SOURCE B: Arthur Barraclough speaking about 'going over the top' and how he believed his **faith** kept him safe. Arthur died in 2004 aged 106.

 KEY WORDS

bayonet
faith
fear
No Man's Land
shrapnel

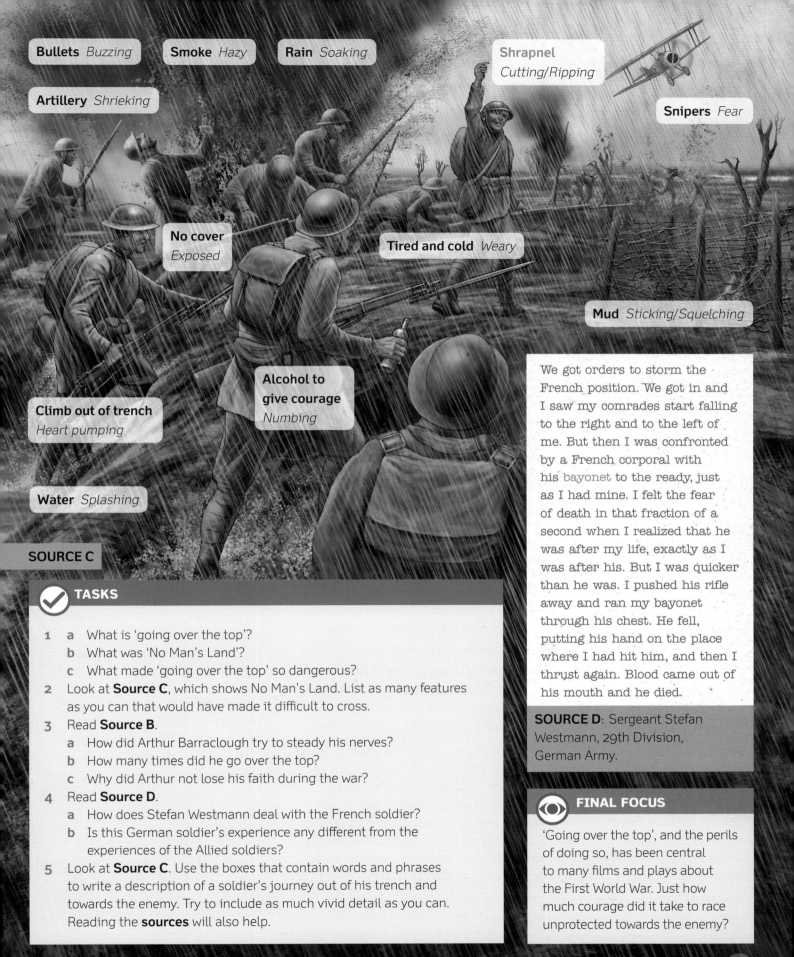

Bullets *Buzzing*

Smoke *Hazy*

Rain *Soaking*

Shrapnel *Cutting/Ripping*

Snipers *Fear*

Artillery *Shrieking*

No cover *Exposed*

Tired and cold *Weary*

Mud *Sticking/Squelching*

Alcohol to give courage *Numbing*

Climb out of trench *Heart pumping*

Water *Splashing*

SOURCE C

We got orders to storm the French position. We got in and I saw my comrades start falling to the right and to the left of me. But then I was confronted by a French corporal with his bayonet to the ready, just as I had mine. I felt the fear of death in that fraction of a second when I realized that he was after my life, exactly as I was after his. But I was quicker than he was. I pushed his rifle away and ran my bayonet through his chest. He fell, putting his hand on the place where I had hit him, and then I thrust again. Blood came out of his mouth and he died.

SOURCE D: Sergeant Stefan Westmann, 29th Division, German Army.

✔ TASKS

1   a   What is 'going over the top'?
     b   What was 'No Man's Land'?
     c   What made 'going over the top' so dangerous?

2   Look at **Source C**, which shows No Man's Land. List as many features as you can that would have made it difficult to cross.

3   Read **Source B**.
     a   How did Arthur Barraclough try to steady his nerves?
     b   How many times did he go over the top?
     c   Why did Arthur not lose his faith during the war?

4   Read **Source D**.
     a   How does Stefan Westmann deal with the French soldier?
     b   Is this German soldier's experience any different from the experiences of the Allied soldiers?

5   Look at **Source C**. Use the boxes that contain words and phrases to write a description of a soldier's journey out of his trench and towards the enemy. Try to include as much vivid detail as you can. Reading the **sources** will also help.

👁 FINAL FOCUS

'Going over the top', and the perils of doing so, has been central to many films and plays about the First World War. Just how much courage did it take to race unprotected towards the enemy?

3.4 A letter from the front

OBJECTIVES
- Explain what types of letter came back from the front.
- Analyse the messages that were in the letters.
- Explain why some letters had a hidden meaning.

Look at this photo. It shows soldiers in the trenches receiving letters from home. Letters would give the soldiers hope and allow them to escape briefly from the boredom and horrors of trench warfare. Many soldiers sent letters home as well, so that friends and family could find out how they were getting on. What do you think it would have been like to receive a letter from the front?

KEY WORDS

censorship
Dead Man's Penny

SOURCE A: An officer distributes letters from home to the troops at Christmas – location unknown.

Second Lt Trevor Bird's letter: Christmas Day, 1914

My Dear Father

Christmas Day you see me still alive, though by Jove, since the 20th I've been having a fairly hairy time. We were sent to a place where the Germans had broken the line. When we finally got under the last cover available we were ordered to make a bayonet attack on the German trenches! It was a criminal order on the part of the man who ordered it.

After 26 hours in water up to the waist I was sent to dry myself with my half squadron behind the firing line. Still sopping wet we were sent off to another lot of trenches and from these I was then pulled out and sent off for a patrol. Every time I showed myself 'ping' went a bullet!

However, I finally reached the line of the British Trenches I was making for where to cap all my troubles, I was arrested as a German spy!! It was not until I had been taken before the C.O., with a rifle muzzle in the small of my back, that I was allowed to depart. Yesterday, we did a 25-mile [40km] march I have a pair of feet like balloons and an attack of neuritis and a chill! [...] My tootsies are awfully painful. Well we get well paid so mustn't complain I suppose. Must stop now, so once more wishing you a Merry Christmas and Happy New Year.

Au revoir – Your Loving Trevor

SOURCE B: An uncensored letter home from Trevor Bird in 1914.

CENSORSHIP

One of the problems soldiers faced when sending a letter home was that it may have been censored before it got there. This involved certain parts of the letter being cut out by the authorities, in case it fell into enemy hands or gave an unfavourable impression of the war.

The sorts of things that would be censored included:

- specific details, including the location of troops
- descriptions of hard living conditions
- information that might help the enemy.

Source B was written by Trevor Bird, a Second Lieutenant, to his father. It somehow managed to escape being censored, and his father received the whole letter.

THE LETTER NO ONE WANTED

There was a type of letter, or telegram, that was dreaded by families. This was an official notice from the War Office stating that somebody had been killed in action. Sometimes, an officer from the front would also write a more personal letter, as is shown in **Source C**.

SOURCE C: A personal letter to a widow from her late husband's commanding officer.

On behalf of the Officers and men of my Company I wish to offer you my sincere sympathy in the bereavement you have sustained in the death of your husband. I feel that you would like to know that your husband had the goodwill & esteem of all his comrades & his loss was felt with general sorrow by the Company.

Your husband was mortally wounded on 16th Sept. by a bomb from an enemy aeroplane. He received immediate medical attention but died almost immediately and as he was unconscious I am sure that he suffered no pain … [details of burial] … If there is anything you would like to know or that I can do to help you, I shall be only too pleased to do so.

Again assuring you of all our sympathy with you and your little girl

I remain, Yours Sincerely Edgar H. Collcutt Capt. RE

 FINAL FOCUS

John Roberts, pictured here and named on the 'Dead Man's Penny' in **Source D**, is a relation of a member of staff who works at The Swinton High School in Manchester. Do you have a family member who served in the First World War? Can you do some research to find out if you have?

SOURCE E: John Roberts.

SOURCE D: When a soldier died, the family received a **Dead Man's Penny**, which had the soldier's name inscribed. This was also accompanied by a letter from Buckingham Palace.

TASKS

1 a What types of letter were sent during the First World War?
   b What does **censorship** mean?
   c Why were letters censored?
2 Read **Source B**. Imagine you are a government official who has been given the task of censoring the letter. What would you cut out? Why?
3 Read **Source C**.
   a How do you feel reading the letter?
   b How is it written? For example, how has the author tried to 'soften the blow'?

4 Look at **Source D**.
   a What is the inscription on the Dead Man's Penny?
   b How would you feel to receive this penny, along with the letter?
   c Today it is possible to buy Dead Man's Pennies on the Internet. Why do you think so many families have parted with these tokens?

3.5 Gallipoli

OBJECTIVES
- Explain why Gallipoli was invaded and what happened there.
- Judge whether Gallipoli was a success or a failure.

KEY WORDS

ANZAC
Dardanelles
Ottoman

SOURCE B: A map showing Gallipoli at the entrance to the Dardanelles and the Black Sea.

SOURCE A: Troops coming ashore at Gallipoli.

The First World War is most widely associated with trench warfare on the Western Front in France and Belgium. But the war was much more widely fought than this. One of the areas that saw fierce fighting was the **Dardanelles,** a vital route for trade and shipping, guarding the entrance to the Black Sea. By holding the Dardanelles a nation could block trade to Russia through the Ukraine and dominate a vital part of the Mediterranean.

THE PLAN OF ATTACK

By attacking the Gallipoli peninsula the British hoped that they would be able to quickly knock Turkey out of the war, reducing pressure on Russia's army and allowing her to concentrate on the war with Germany. Their primary aim was to attack Constantinople and take out the Turkish defences, which consisted of mines and large pieces of artillery.

Troops from Australia and New Zealand, Turkey, France and Great Britain were involved in the attack on Gallipoli. The expected easy victory did not happen, however. They met great resistance from the Turkish (Ottoman) armies and the war in Gallipoli quickly became a war in trenches, very much like the war on the Western Front. After eight months it became a costly withdrawal.

STOP THE CLOCK

The **Ottoman** 'Turkish' Empire entered the war in November 1914.

The Australian and New Zealand forces landed on Gallipoli on 25 April, meeting fierce resistance from the Ottoman Turkish defenders. What had been planned as a bold stroke to knock Turkey out of the war quickly became a stalemate, and the campaign dragged on for eight months. At the end of 1915 the allied forces were evacuated, after both sides had suffered heavy casualties and endured great hardships. Over 8,000 Australian soldiers had been killed. News of the landing on Gallipoli had made a profound impact on Australians at home, and 25 April soon became the day on which Australians remembered the sacrifice of those who had died in the war.

SOURCE E: From the Australian War Memorial website.

Those heroes that shed their blood and lost their lives... You are now lying in the soil of a friendly country. Therefore rest in peace. There is no difference between the Johnnies and the Mehmets to us where they lie side by side here in this country of ours... You, the mothers, who sent their sons from far away countries wipe away your tears; your sons are now lying in our bosom and are in peace. After having lost their lives on this land they have become our sons as well.

SOURCE F: Mustafa Kemal Ataturk, founder and first president of the Turkish Republic, in a tribute to the fallen ANZACs of Gallipoli.

SOURCE C: Prime Minister of Australia, Mr W.M. Hughes, addresses soldiers who were wounded at Gallipoli.

SOURCE D: An **ANZAC** soldier carries a wounded comrade at Gallipoli.

INTERPRETATIONS OF GALLIPOLI

1 It was a failure – they did not manage to knock Turkey out of the war.
2 Churchill resigned as First Lord of the Admiralty after the failed attack.
3 A new government and a new prime minister came into power after the Gallipoli landings – was that because of the failure at Gallipoli?
4 Many troops were evacuated safely from the Gallipoli peninsula.
5 It was a representation of Australian independence as a new nation.
6 It forced the Allies to seek an end to the war in Belgium and France, rather than looking elsewhere.

 FINAL FOCUS

Why do you think Gallipoli is not as widely remembered as some of the battles on the Western Front?

✓ TASKS

1 a Where is Gallipoli?
   b Why was there a battle there?
   c What are the Dardanelles?

2 Read **Source E**.
   a When did the Gallipoli landings take place?
   b How many Australian troops were killed?
   c How long did the fighting last for?

3 Look at **Source D** and conduct some research. What were the conditions like at Gallipoli? What would it have been like to fight there?

4 a Look at **Interpretations of Gallipoli**. Read each interpretation and sort them into a table with two columns headed 'positive' and 'negative'.
   b Was Gallipoli a success or a failure? Write a paragraph to explain your thinking.

5 Read **Source F**, the speech made by Mustafa Kemal Ataturk.
   a What is the point that he is making?
   b How important is that point in your opinion?

3.6 What happened at the Somme?

OBJECTIVES
- Describe what happened at the Battle of the Somme.
- Analyse the view of a historian about the Battle of the Somme.

'Bloody' battles are what people remember most about the First World War. One such battle is the Battle of the Somme, perhaps the bloodiest battle of the whole war. On these pages, you'll find different boxes containing information about the battle. Your job is to analyse the information, and build a picture of what happened.

SOURCE A: British troops make their way towards the enemy during the Battle of the Somme.

WHY DID THE BATTLE HAPPEN?

At 7:30am on 1 July 1916, the Allies began an attack on enemy trenches that were positioned near the River Somme in France. The following battle lasted for 140 days. The purpose of the battle was to capture completely the German trenches at Beaumont Hamel. Before they started, the British and French spent a week heavily firing shells and detonating mines to destroy the German line. The idea was that, when it came to the start of the battle, the Germans would already be vastly weakened.

WHAT HAPPENED NEXT?

In June 1916, we were rushed to France for a big attack, to liberate the French at Verdun. They were getting a real doing, and we had to make a diversion. At the start we were lined up ready to go over, at the whistle, at half seven. A huge mine went off to the right. It went off too soon, and it gave the Germans a chance to come out of their deep dugouts and concentrate on us. I think they were surprised to see us walking. In our orders, we had to walk across. We had been led to believe by 'higher ups' that the big **bombardment**, over the days and nights, had obliterated the enemy. But we knew it hadn't because their positions were so strong. Their dugouts were way down under the

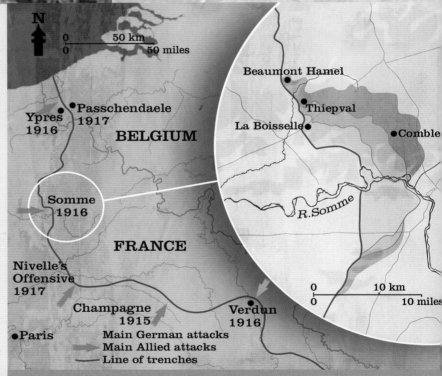

SOURCE B: The trench line in France and Belgium (1915–1917) and the limited ground captured during the Battle of the Somme.

parapets of the trenches, and they couldn't be reached by artillery fire. All they did was to wait down there until our barrage lifted, and then they came up to have some target practice at us. We were held up by huge coils of barbed wire, and in the odd gap that we made for, we were greeted by their heavy machine guns.

SOURCE C: Private Frank Lindlay, 14th Battalion, York and Lancaster Regiment, describes his experiences of the Somme.

IMPORTANT FACTS

- The German trenches were well designed and had numerous deep shelters.
- Many shells failed to explode, and those designed to cut all the barbed wire protecting the German lines weren't up to the job.
- The German forces had learned from previous attacks: major bombardments usually ended just before the British troops went over the top, so, when the week-long shelling stopped, the Germans rushed from their shelters, put machine guns in position and were ready and waiting.
- The British soldiers, many of whom were those who had volunteered in 1914 and 1915, had never faced real battle before.
- British soldiers met fierce resistance from the German troops.

SOURCE E: A famous still taken from the film 'The Battle of the Somme'. What is happening in this picture? Why do you think it has become so famous?

40,000 wounded on first day

20,000 dead on first day

415,000 British casualties in total

200,000 French casualties in total

600,000 German casualties in total

Allies had advanced their front lines **5 miles (8km)**

Beaumont Hamel was captured in **November 1916**

SOURCE D: Statistics showing the outcome of the battle.

 STOP THE CLOCK

1 July 1916 was the day the British Army suffered 60,000 casualties in the Battle of the Somme.

 FINAL FOCUS

Many people have different opinions and **interpretations** of the same event or actions. Why do some people view the Battle of the Somme as a disaster?

KEY WORDS

bombardment

 TASKS

1 Using the information and sources on these pages, copy and fill in the following table:

Where did the Battle of the Somme take place?	
When did it happen?	
Who was fighting whom?	
What were the aims of the battle?	
How long did the battle last?	

2 Read **Source C**.
   a What had Private Frank Lindlay been led to believe by 'higher ups'? Note down all of the 'expectations' of the British Army that you can find.
   b What orders were the soldiers given?
   c Why were the 'higher ups' mistaken?
   d What happened to many of the soldiers?

3 Look at **Source E**. Write creatively about the outcomes of the Battle of the Somme from this soldier's perspective. Use the statistics in **Source D** to help you.

3.7 How good a leader was Haig?

OBJECTIVES
- Explain who Douglas Haig was and his role in the war.
- Analyse different **interpretations** about how good a leader he was.

Douglas Haig led the troops at the Battle of the Somme and at many other key battles of the First World War. When the war started, Haig was already a highly respected military leader, as he had lots of experience of conflict across the globe. However, because the Battle of the Somme involved so much bloodshed, **opinions** about Haig are divided. Was it his fault that the battle caused such a huge loss of life? And how good a leader was he really?

 KEY WORDS

interpretations
opinions

SOURCE A: How would you describe Haig? What do his clothes tell you about him?

SOURCE B: The front cover of a biography of Haig, written by Sir John Davidson, Haig's Director of Operations from 1916 onwards. Davidson's book describes Haig's tactics in detail, and proclaims him as 'Master of the field'.

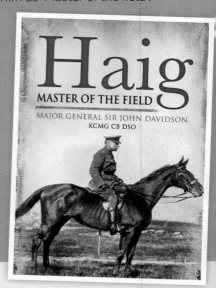

IMPORTANT FACTS

1. More British soldiers died in this war than any other war before it.
2. There were 415,000 British casualties during the Battle of the Somme.
3. Haig was learning as he went along – no one had experienced a war like this.
4. The quality of weapons at the time limited the possibility of war without casualties.
5. Haig was generally well regarded during the war.
6. Britain and its allies won the war.
7. Haig campaigned for veterans to be looked after when the war had finished.
8. Some politicians, including David Lloyd George, were critical of Haig's out-of-date tactics.

A MILITARY LIFE

Field Marshal Douglas Haig (1861–1928) served in the Boer Wars (1899–1902) and many other military campaigns during his lifetime. He was involved in leading the British Expeditionary Force (BEF) during the First World War, and led the troops during several key battles, including the Battle of the Somme. Although his military experience and tactical skill was highly regarded (see **Source B**), it is argued that during the Battle he misjudged the effectiveness of the early bombardments against German defences, and he continued to send British soldiers to their deaths, for little territorial gain. The sources on these pages present different opinions. Which are the most convincing?

Though he had no more idea than others how to win the war, he was sure that he could win it… This unshakeable confidence, and the support of the king, enabled Haig to survive a long record of failure and to emerge in the end victorious… Haig had to do what he did and, though he did not succeed, no one better was found to take his place.

SOURCE C: Historian A.J.P. Taylor defending Haig in *The First World War* (1963).

SOURCE E: Cartoon from *Punch* magazine, 1917.

Major-General (addressing the men before practising an attack behind the lines). "I want you to understand that there is a difference between a rehearsal and the real thing. There are three essential differences; first, the absence of the enemy. Now (*turning to the Regimental Sergeant-Major*) what is the second difference?" *Sergeant-Major.* "The absence of the General, Sir."

SOURCE F: Haig's funeral procession in 1928 had a full guard of honour, and became a day of national mourning. What does this treatment tell you about Haig?

8 PEOPLE OF WWI: DAVID LLOYD GEORGE

David Lloyd George was Prime Minister from 1916 and was particularly critical of Haig. He had a big influence on public opinion.

> *... he did not possess the necessary breadth of vision or imagination to plan a great campaign against some of the ablest generals of the war. I never met a man in a high position who seemed to me so utterly devoid of imagination.*

SOURCE D: Lloyd George writing in *War Memoirs* (1928).

FINAL FOCUS

People forming their own **interpretation** of events and people in history is important. What is your own interpretation of Haig?

 TASKS

1. a Who was Haig?
   b What experience did Haig have of warfare?
   c What was Haig's role in the First World War?
2. Why do people disagree about how good a leader Haig was?
3. Copy and complete the following table for each of the sources on these pages. Work in small groups.

Source	Is it for or against Haig, or neither? How do you know?	How reliable is this source? (i.e. can we trust it?)
A		
B		

4. a Use your table, and the 'important facts' box on the opposite page, to create two lists of arguments – one 'for' and one 'against' Haig as a good leader.
   b Put your arguments in order, with the most convincing at the top.
   c Which arguments are the most convincing – 'for', or 'against'?
5. Choose a side of the argument, and prepare to debate it. Decide on your key points, and how you will argue them. (Remember, a good debater will try to predict the arguments that might come from the other side!)

GCSE-STYLE QUESTION

'Haig was a "Butcher".' How far do you agree?

3.8 Shot at dawn

OBJECTIVES
- Explain what is meant by 'shot at dawn'.
- Decide whether you believe it was wrong to shoot people who refused to fight.
- Make a judgement about whether the soldiers should have been pardoned in 2006.

Do you know what the word **coward** means? How would you define it? The reality of the war was terrifying for many soldiers on the front line, and at times many would have wanted to run away from it all. If you were a leader in the British Army, this was a problem. They couldn't have men abandoning their posts or weakening the resolve of other men. So what do you do if people refuse to fight? How can you prevent **mutiny**? And how can you tell the difference between someone who is trying to avoid doing their duty, and someone who needs medical help for their mental health?

SOURCE A: A soldier suffering from shell shock has his 'frozen' ankles manipulated to help him walk. Some of the men who were shot at dawn displayed symptoms of shell shock.

COURT MARTIAL

Keeping an army in check and obedient to orders in the face of great hostility is very difficult. The policy that was adopted during the First World War was that men who were cowards, or **deserters**, were shot after a **court martial** – a kind of military trial. In total, 306 men were 'shot at dawn' by the British Army. There were several different reasons why men might be shot (see **Source B**).

KEY WORDS

court martial
coward
deserter
mutiny
pardon
posthumous

STOP THE CLOCK

306 soldiers who had been 'shot at dawn' as cowards were given a **pardon** by the British Government in 2006.

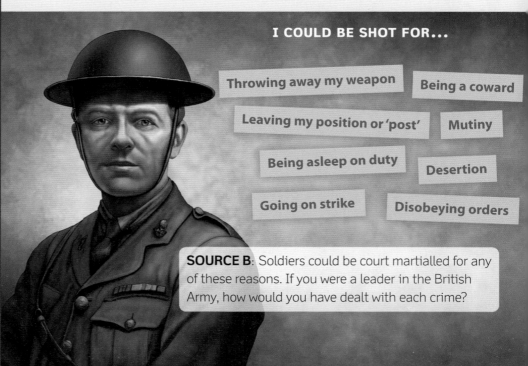

I COULD BE SHOT FOR...

Throwing away my weapon   Being a coward

Leaving my position or 'post'   Mutiny

Being asleep on duty   Desertion

Going on strike   Disobeying orders

SOURCE B: Soldiers could be court martialled for any of these reasons. If you were a leader in the British Army, how would you have dealt with each crime?

DIFFERING VIEWS

Look at **Source A**. One of the reasons why many people have argued against the 306 executions is that a number of the men displayed symptoms of shell shock. This means that they might have deserted their posts because they needed medical attention, not because they were cowards. Others disagree and argue that rules during warfare need to be harsh, and we shouldn't judge the decisions that were made then against the standards of today. Read the following sources for different arguments on this issue.

> Those soldiers should never have been shot for what they did. They were mentally ill – scared stiff and afraid that they would be killed. Some had been fighting for years. One indiscretion and they lost their lives! They should all be pardoned and given proper burials with their names recorded alongside all the other soldiers of the Great War.

SOURCE D: William Jones – amateur historian and ex-soldier.

> Corelli Barnett, a military historian, said last night that the **posthumous** pardon was 'pointless' after all these years. These were decisions taken in the heat of a war when the commanders' primary duty was to keep the army together and to keep it fighting. They were therefore decisions taken from a different moral perspective, he said. For the people of this generation to come along and second-guess decisions taken then is wrong. It was done in a particular historical setting and in a particular moral and social climate. It's pointless to give these pardons. What's the point of a posthumous pardon?

SOURCE E: Ben Fenton, writing for *The Telegraph* in 2006.

SOURCE C: The 'shot at dawn' memorial in Staffordshire.

 PEOPLE OF WWI

Harry Farr is one of the more famous from among the 306 casualties. Farr fought in the trenches on the Western Front, but in 1915 he was taken to hospital with severe convulsions. He was sent back to fight in the Battle of the Somme. On 17 September he went missing, and when he was found he refused to return to the front line. He was found guilty of cowardice and executed on 18 October 1916. His family campaigned for his name to be cleared for many years, resulting in the 2006 **pardon**.

 TASKS

1. **a** What does the phrase 'shot at dawn' refer to?
    b For what crimes could a soldier be shot at dawn?
    c How many soldiers were shot at dawn in total in the First World War?
2. Discuss with a partner: why would an army shoot some of its own men?
3. In your pairs, look at **Sources B** to **E**.
    a Write down all of the arguments for and against the actions of the British Army.
    b Decide which argument is the most convincing, and which is the least convincing.
4. Write a letter to Corelli Barnett, the historian mentioned in **Source E**. What would you say to him about his opinion?
5. Do some research and choose one of the men who was shot at dawn. What can you find out about him? Why was he shot?
6. Imagine you were on the 2006 pardoning committee. Prepare two paragraphs explaining whether or not you would recommend the men be pardoned.

 FINAL FOCUS

As historians, should we judge the decisions that were made in the First World War by today's standards? What is your opinion?

4.1 Weapons of war

Gas! Gas! Quick, boys! – An ecstasy of fumbling,
Fitting the clumsy helmets just in time;
But someone still was yelling out and stumbling,
And flound'ring like a man in fire or lime …
Dim, through the misty panes and thick green
light, As under a green sea, I saw him drowning.
In all my dreams, before my helpless sight,
He plunges at me, guttering, choking, drowning.

SOURCE A: From the poem 'Dulce et Decorum est' by Wilfred Owen.

POISON GAS

During the course of the war the Germans got through 68,000 tonnes of poison gas and the British 51,000 tonnes. Different types of poison gas were used – either blown by the wind towards the enemy or fired at them in shells. The effects on victims of a gas attack ranged from choking, nausea and blurred vision, to blistering skin, blindness and heart failure. Despite the fear factor, only about 10 per cent of all who were gassed died from their injuries, although many suffered from the effects for the rest of their lives. Gas accounted for around 4 per cent of all combat deaths in the First World War. In comparison, artillery fire accounted for between 60 and 70 per cent. The three main types of poison gas were **chlorine** gas, Mustard gas and **phosgene** gas.

TRENCH CLUBS

A club or truncheon used to bludgeon the enemy at close range. Good if you got that close.

SOURCE C: A German trench club.

SOURCE B: A British protective gas helmet; soldiers would breathe in through the nose and out through the tube at their mouth.

Stalemate on the Western Front led to both sides developing new technological weapons aiming to break through the enemy's frontline. Development of existing weapons like machine guns and submarines sped up, whilst new weapons (like the tank) were used on land, in the sea or in the air. Some weapons were **offensive** (for attacking), whereas others were **defensive** (stopped enemy attacks).

 KEY WORDS

chlorine
grenade
phosgene
projector

TANKS

The first tanks made an appearance at the Battle of the Somme in September 1916. These cumbersome new offensive weapons managed a top speed of 0.5mph (0.8kmph) and took four men to steer them. Although they did in some cases instill fear into German defenders, in military terms they were not a war-winning solution to the stalemate.

SOURCE D

GRENADES

One of the most effective offensive weapons of the war was the **grenade**. This small bomb gave the frontline soldier a good deal of destructive power. They were often referred to as 'Mills Bombs'.

> The grenade – a hand-thrown bomb detonated by impact or a time fuse – was only widely issued to German forces in 1914. The British had almost none until Spring 1915, and their first Mills Mark II grenades often exploded in the hand of the thrower. It was not until 1916, with the Mark III, that such accidents were reduced to 1 in 20,000.

SOURCE F: H.P. Willmott writing in *World War 1* (2007).

SOURCE E: A 'Mills Bomb' hand grenade.

SOURCE G: Soldiers using a Lewis gun.

MACHINE GUNS

Machine guns were deadly because of the speed at which they could fire bullets. Used defensively, a well-placed machine gun could mow down lines of advancing troops in minutes. Early machine guns, such as the Maxim, were heavy and needed two or three men to operate them. As the war progressed, the British developed the Lewis gun, which could be carried and fired by just one man.

SOURCE H

LIVENS PROJECTOR – FLAME-THROWER

The Livens **projector** was a huge flame-thrower that was used at the Battle of the Somme. Troops in the trenches often used much smaller flame-throwers as well (see **Source H**).

> From a small, concealed nozzle on the surface, the 'weapon of terror' spewed flames over a range of 300 feet [91m]. As the nozzle pivoted, the jet raked along the German frontline, pouring blazing oil onto the enemy position.

SOURCE I: Jasper Copping in *The Telegraph*, May 2010.

✓ TASKS

1 Using the information about each weapon on these pages, copy and complete the table below.

Weapon	Description (what does it do? Is it offensive or defensive or both?)	Rating out of 10, where 10 is highly effective in the war and 0 is not at all effective. Explain your rating.
Poison Gas		

2 Using your table and extra research, put together a booklet aimed at younger students entitled 'Weapons of the First World War'.

3 Read the poem extract in **Source A**. Was this written by a supporter of the war or an opponent of the war? Explain your thinking.

GCSE-STYLE QUESTION

'New technological weapons in WWI, like the tank, were little more than a distraction from the real fighting by soldiers in the trenches.' Use your knowledge and sources to explain how far you agree with this interpretation.

 FINAL FOCUS

Why do you think armies used different types of weapon?

4.2 A war underground

OBJECTIVES
- Explain what the war underground was.
- Describe how and why it was fought.
- Judge how significant the war underground was.

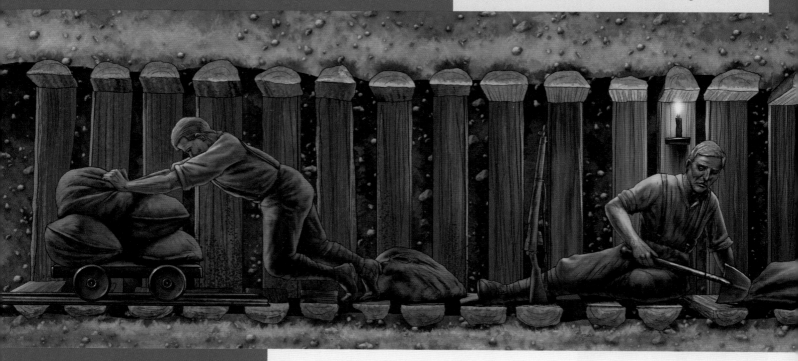

Few people realize that below the battlefields are a vast network of tunnels, shelters and mineshafts that were dug out by dedicated tunnellers. These tunnellers – or **clay-kickers** – fought their battles underground, risking death under tonnes of earth rather than from machine guns and shells above ground.

UNDERGROUND EXPLOSIVES

As war in the trenches reached a stalemate, people looked for other ways to penetrate enemy defences. Blowing up trenches from underneath, although extremely dangerous, seemed one way to attack without the loss of life that was often involved in 'going over the top'.

Mining was often undertaken by the **Royal Engineers** or by ex-miners. Very little training was given, and the miners had to rely on ingenuity to work out the best mining methods. They worked in terrible conditions, enduring flooding, extreme cold and poor light (usually with only a candle to see by).

STAYING UNDETECTED

Work had to be carried out as quietly as possible to avoid detection. Many listening devices were developed to detect enemy miners, including a stick that was held between the teeth to feel for any vibrations. There was always a high risk of tunnels and shafts collapsing, and, of course, of coming across the enemy mining towards you.

SOURCE A: An officer in a tunnel listening for signs of the enemy.

KEY WORDS

clay-kicker
Royal Engineers
mole

The Manchester tunnelers, nicknamed **moles**, used a technique called clay-kicking to dig through the terrain. The digger would sit at a 45 degree angle with his back against a wooden frame and his feet facing the digging surface. Using a grafting tool that was a kind of combination pogo stick/spade/posthole digger, he would drive the tool into the soil by pushing with his feet on its crossbar, then pass it over his head to a 'bagger' who would put the spoil in sandbags so a third worker could get it out on a little hand-cranked trolley. On his way back, the trolley handler would bring in more timber to shore up the tunnel. This process was fast and it was quiet. The Germans were using pickaxes to dig their tunnels, not exactly the best tools for clay removal and by their very nature percussively loud.

SOURCE B: A modern historian's account of clay-kicking.

The whole earth heaved and flared, a tremendous and magnificent column rose up into the sky. There was an ear-splitting roar, drowning all the guns, flinging the machine sideways in the repercussing air. The earth column rose higher and higher to almost 4000 feet [1.2km].

SOURCE C: The account of a British pilot who witnessed the explosion of a huge mine at La Boiselle on 1 July 1916. Today, its crater is visited by 75,000 people touring the area every year.

DISADVANTAGES

The work of miners was often overlooked by high-ranking leaders in the army. Mines took a long time to dig, and progress depended on what type of earth they were dug in. Harder ground, such as chalk, might take twice as long to dig through as clay. Not only this but the miners had to be digging in front of their own infantry. If the men above ground suddenly surged forwards, the mine became closer to the infantry than was safe. Mines could be a good tactic, but only if they were meticulously planned.

 PEOPLE OF WWI

The man behind the mining plan was John Norton-Griffiths. He had previously helped build the London sewer system, and was experienced with heavy clay soils. He was therefore thought to be the perfect candidate to overcome the challenges of tunnelling under the enemy.

 TASKS

1 a What was the nickname given to the miners who dug the tunnels?
   b Why were the tunnels dug?
   c What conditions did the miners have to put up with?
2 Use the images of the tunnellers and the information on these pages to write a description of their role in the war. Use **Source B** to add more detail.
3 a Read **Source C**. What does the source suggest about the power of the mines? How does the writer achieve this?
   b Add a beginning and an end to **Source C**, using your imagination and creative writing.
4 Many of the Generals underestimated the value of the tunnellers. Why?
5 Why was mining not seen as a more viable weapon? Construct a table of positive and negative points about using mining as a weapon.

 FINAL FOCUS

What have you learned about the tactics and expertise of the British Army?

4.3 A war at sea

OBJECTIVES
- Explain why the war at sea was so important.
- Describe the U-boat threat.
- Evaluate the effectiveness of the methods used to tackle the U-boat threat.

When thinking about war, many people do not consider that control of the seas may be important. Today, food and goods can be flown into countries so that essential supplies do not run out. During the First World War, this was not as easy, and control of the seas meant that countries could be kept supplied and people would not have to face starvation. The war at sea was fought primarily in the North Sea and the Atlantic, but battles also took place in the Dardanelles off the coast of Turkey, and off the Falkland Islands. If Britain had not been able to take control of the seas, it might also have faced invasion by Germany.

KEY WORDS

convoy
shipping
sloop
supply
trawler
U-boat

SOURCE A: A U-boat. Was this the greatest new weapon?

PEOPLE OF WWI

At sea. We are now in the zone of submarine activity and the usual precautions are being taken. The ships have been zig-zagging all day. Some of the ships are going to French ports, the rest to East Coast ports. Most of the cargoes consist of copper, aeroplane parts and other necessary munition and fighting machinery.

SOURCE B: A diary entry on 14 July 1917 by Harry Richard Tothill, a Sick Berth Steward on HMS *Roxburgh*.

WHAT IS A U-BOAT?

A U-boat is a German submarine. U-boat is a shortened version of *Unterseeboot* – or undersea boat. These vessels were ideal for 'sneaking up' on the enemy and attacking while remaining unseen. However, submarines were not only available to the Germans – many were also available to the British and were used to devastating effect by both sides during the war.

HOW MUCH OF A PROBLEM WERE THEY?

The U-boats were a real threat to **shipping** and merchant vessels, in particular those bringing essential supplies from America. These supplies were keeping Britain going during the war, as a small island nation like the UK was unable to grow all the essential food supplies that it needed, while also having to **supply** the war effort. U-boat attacks caused major disruption to this supply chain and eventually meant that rationing had to be introduced in 1918.

SOURCE C: Men on a navy **trawler**, which were sometimes armed to defend the fishing boats from enemy submarines or aircraft.

NEW RULES

The submarine changed the rules of warfare. Boats would usually give a warning before an attack, but submarines relied on the element of surprise. The German leaders did not use U-boats to their full potential until 1917 when they began unrestricted submarine warfare. Attacks on all supplies carried by ship to Britain increased and this had a devastating effect on American trade with Britain.

In 1915 an American passenger ship, the *Lusitania*, was struck by a submarine torpedo and sank. America urged Germany to stop its submarine attacks. Germany's refusal led to the declaration of war on Germany by America in April 1917. America's entry into the war meant valuable new armies of American soldiers were sent to the Western Front from early 1918. Combined with the increased use of aircraft, tanks and new tactics of attack, the end of the war was at last in sight.

Some 370 U-boats were built by the Germans in the First World War; of which 178 were lost, and nearly 5000 men; they sank 5708 ships totalling over 11 million tons. The ravages British shipping sustained in the years 1914–18 inflicted by German U-boats remained seared on the British mind long after the end of the conflict.

SOURCE D: Statistics from historian Michael Gunton in *Dive! Dive! Dive! Submarines at War* (2003).

HOW TO TACKLE A SUBMARINE

To combat the threat of the submarines, new methods had to be devised. During the war the following tactics, among many others, helped to sink 178 U-boats.

1 Q-boats – disguise heavily armed boats as decoys and allow the U-boats to target them. The Q-boats would then open fire.
2 **Convoy** system – merchant vessels would travel in convoy, protected by Royal Navy ships.
3 Aircraft – U-boats could often be seen from the sky.
4 Use anti-submarine vessels (**sloops**) to specifically target the U-boats.
5 Set up nets to catch the submarines in.
6 Lay mines to blow up the submarines.
7 Use a 'hydrophone' to listen for submarines and to warn people.
8 British ships were forbidden to pick up survivors if travelling in a convoy so that they would not be open to further attacks.
9 Use 'depth charges' – bombs that would explode deep below the surface.

 FINAL FOCUS

What would have happened if the war at sea had carried on? What would have happened to UK food supplies?

 TASKS

1 a What is a U-boat?
  b What is 'U-boat' an abbreviation of?
  c Which American liner was sunk by a U-boat?
2 Read **Source D**.
  a How many German U-boats were built?
  b How many were sunk?
  c How much shipping did they sink?
3 List five ways the British tackled the U-boat threat.
4 Look at the proposed methods for tackling submarines. You have been asked to make a decision on which two methods would be most effective. Which ones would you choose and why? Come up with positives and negatives for each method.

5 Read **Source B**.
  a Who has written this?
  b What type of boat are they on? What would it be used for?
  c How is this boat avoiding submarines?
6 Write a top-secret report for the British Government into the U-boat threat. Outline the problems and how they could be combated.

GCSE-STYLE QUESTION

Explain why it was essential that the U-Boat threat was stopped.

4.4 A war in the air

OBJECTIVES
- Describe the role that **aircraft** and pilots played in the war.
- Explain why being a pilot was so dangerous.
- Make a judgment about why pilots were often seen as heroes.

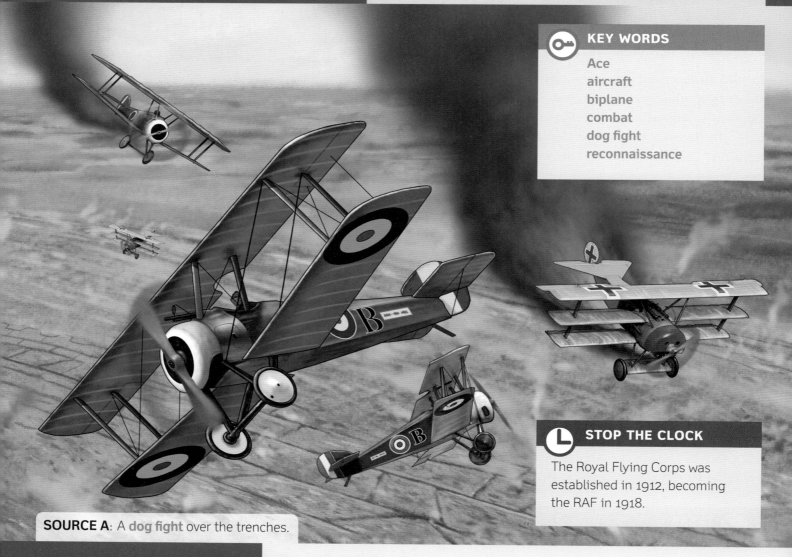

KEY WORDS

Ace
aircraft
biplane
combat
dog fight
reconnaissance

STOP THE CLOCK

The Royal Flying Corps was established in 1912, becoming the RAF in 1918.

SOURCE A: A **dog fight** over the trenches.

Aircraft were still relatively new when the First World War started. In 1914 there was little actual understanding of how to use aircraft effectively in **combat**. Initially aircraft were used for **reconnaissance** (observation). They improved the accuracy of artillery fire on the ground. However, as the war progressed, aircraft took on an increasingly important role.

BATTLES IN THE SKY

The early planes were mainly one- or two-seater **biplanes** that now look very flimsy compared to the planes of the Second World War. It would take great courage to fly them over the trenches and No Man's Land. Pilots who had shot down more than five enemy aircraft were known as **Ace** pilots, and were the heroes of the air.

Almost as soon as rival aircraft met, their pilots were using rifles and revolvers against each other. There was soon pressure to improve technology so that fighter aircraft could be more effective. By the end of 1915, aircraft were being used on both sides to fight battles in the sky, equipped with machine guns and bombs. The sky over the trenches of the Western Front saw frequent dog fights (see **Source A**), as pilots fought for the control of the skies.

THE DANGER OF BEING A PILOT

To become a pilot, men had to join up as pilots at the start of the war or transfer from the army. Regardless of the route to the cockpit, a pilot's life-expectancy was poor. Even if they could have managed to get out of a burning, damaged aircraft, the pilots had no parachutes. Some figures suggest that the average pilot might expect to survive only eight weeks on the front line (not 20 minutes as suggested in the history comedy *Blackadder*!). Some statistics suggest that nearly half of the pilots killed in the First World War may not have been killed by the enemy, but were in fact killed in training.

HONOUR AND REPUTATION

Many pilots from different countries gained a formidable reputation in the air despite such danger. Many became heroes, and their national press used news of their prowess to boost morale at home and among other forces.

SOURCE B: One of the most famous aeroplanes in the Great War was the British Sopwith Camel. It was armed with two machine guns and one bomb that weighed 4.9kg.

SOURCE C: The remains of a German Zeppelin. Can you find out what a Zeppelin was used for?

PEOPLE OF WWI

The Red Baron – Manfred von Richthofen – was Germany's most famous fighter pilot, shooting down a record 80 British, Canadian and Australian airmen. His blood-red Fokker Triplane became legendary and he acquired hero status among the German public, and respect among enemy pilots. He suffered a head injury in July 1917 but, despite medical advice, he returned to the air. He was shot down and killed on 21 April 1918.

SOURCE D: The Red Baron.

TASKS

1   a   When was the Royal Flying Corps established?
    b   What were planes initially used for?
    c   Name an aircraft from the First World War.
2   What dangers did a pilot face in the First World War?
3   Look at **Source A**. Produce a piece of creative writing about this scene, using as many key words as you can.
4   Using the information on these pages – especially **People of WWI** – design a recruitment poster for pilots, encouraging men to join the Royal Flying Corps. What information would you emphasize? What would you leave out?
5   Why were the pilots of the First World War so highly regarded? Write two paragraphs to answer this question, making sure that you refer to evidence from these pages as well as giving your own conclusions.

FINAL FOCUS

Aircraft today are one of the main means of waging war. They provide a relatively safe way for troops to be sent out into war zones. Some planes can even be flown without pilots. What changes have taken place since the First World War?

4.5 Terrible injuries

OBJECTIVES
- Explain the injuries soldiers sustained in the First World War.
- Describe how the soldiers were looked after and made better.
- Analyse a source about the impact of shell shock.

Many soldiers suffered terrible injuries during the Great War. Poison gases could cause burning, choking, lung damage, blindness and, of course, death. Shrapnel could rip open bodies and sever limbs. Machine guns and artillery could inflict injury on a scale never witnessed before.

Common ailments in the trenches included trench foot, trench fever (typhus) and constipation. And that's not to mention exhaustion, and psychological injuries like shell shock.

SOURCE A: American nurses in the trenches, 1918.

SOURCE B: Soldiers blinded during the war mending nets at a recovery facility.

MEDICAL HELP

With so many wounded soldiers, armies set up systems to assess quickly the severity of injuries and then to dispatch patients to first-aid, base hospitals, or hospitals back home. The prime aim was to get soldiers well enough to return to the fighting. More than 75 per cent of wounded British soldiers were sent back to fight.

Many women joined up to serve in the Voluntary Aid Detachment (VAD) and ended up serving on the Western Front. Figures suggest that nearly 40,000 women worked as nurses in close proximity to the battlefields in France and Belgium, with minimal first-aid training. The women who worked in the hospitals, getting men back to full fitness, have sometimes been called the **Roses of No Man's Land**.

PEOPLE OF WWI: HAROLD GILLIES

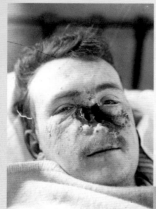
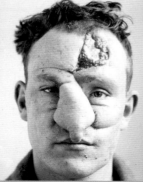

For those who were fortunate enough to have survived their injuries, pioneering **plastic surgery** was often used (see **Source C**). Harold Gillies was a pioneering surgeon who worked on the faces of soldiers who had suffered terrible injuries. His work was the first successful attempt at plastic surgery, and many of his techniques are still used.

SOURCE C: The gradual recovery of William Spreckley, who had his nose shot off in 1917.

SHELL SHOCK

Soldiers in the Great War often had their endurance tested beyond human limits. Conditions in the trenches caused massive stress. Continual shelling, exhaustion and exposure to extreme danger often took their toll on soldiers' minds, although mental illness was not properly understood or recognized at the time. Over 300 British soldiers who suffered from what we now call **shell shock** (a form of nervous breakdown) were accused of cowardice and were court martialled and shot. In total there were 80,000 instances of shell shock suffered by British troops alone during the First World War. Little was known about the illness at the time, but today it is treated as a genuine medical condition and is usually called post-traumatic stress disorder (PTSD).

- The wild fighting type became quiet and moody.
- The sullen type became excitable and talkative.
- The careful type became reckless.
- The well-behaved type became a petty criminal.

Categories of soldiers that were particularly prone to a breakdown were:
- Soldiers over 40 years of age and long service, especially if married.
- Recent reinforcements/drafts of troops fresh from the training battalions.
- Specialists such as: snipers, sappers and tunnellers, machine gunners, tank crews and shock troops.

SOURCE F: Medical trends seen in shell shock victims.

SOURCE D: Some had eyes that would not close.

SOURCE E: Some had convulsions or spasms.

KEY WORDS

plastic surgery
Roses of No Man's Land
shell shock

FINAL FOCUS

Did care of the wounded get better as the war progressed?

TASKS

1 a What injuries did soldiers suffer from in the First World War?
   b What percentage of wounded soldiers were sent back to fight?
   c How and why were women important in the provision of medical help?
2 Look at **Source C**.
   a What happened to William Spreckley?
   b How were his wounds treated?
   c How successful has the doctor been?
3 Using the information on this page, create a medical leaflet on shell shock. Ensure that it answers the following:

   a What is shell shock?
   b What effect does shell shock have on its victims?
   c How were victims of shell shock dealt with during the First World War, and why?
4 Read **Source F** closely, and analyse it, writing in full sentences. Use the following questions to help you:
   a What is this source, and who do you think wrote it?
   b How would you summarize the point the writer is making?
   c What would you say is the 'purpose' of this source?
   d Why do you think certain people were more susceptible to shell shock than others?
   e What questions could you ask about the source?

5.1 A Home Front

Phrases with the word 'front' in them mean somewhere crucial fighting is taking place, for example 'front line' or 'battlefront'. 'The Home Front' suggests people suffered back home in Britain too. There certainly was action in Britain, with air raids, strikes, spies, exploding munitions factories, and hungry people. Unlike in France and Belgium, British women and children died on the Home Front. So how could the battle of the Home Front be won?

OBJECTIVES
- Explain the impact the First World War had on Britain's Home Front.
- Describe some of the problems that the people of Britain overcame.
- Evaluate the role of women during the war.

PEOPLE OF WWI

I was in domestic service and 'hated every minute of it' when war broke out. I was earning £2 a month working from 6:00am to 9:00pm. So when the need came for women 'war workers' my chance came to 'out.' I started on hand-cutting shell fuses ... We worked 12 hours a day ... I thought I was well off earning £5 per week.

SOURCE B: Mrs H.A. Felstead, in 1976, recounting her memories of work during the First World War.

THE ROLE OF WOMEN

Many men volunteered to fight in the Great War, so women had to step up and take their places in many ways. With over 1 million men in the army by Christmas 1914, women assumed that they would be needed. Yet it was not until 1915, after the women had held a 'right to work' march, that the government began to see the value of female workers. Approximately 250,000 women were employed in the Women's Land Army alone, and many others in nursing, driving and mining work. The most well-known sector in which women were employed was **munitions** – making bombs, guns and bullets. Around 1 million women were employed in munitions work and were nicknamed 'munitionettes' or canaries. They got the nickname of canaries because some women's skin would turn a yellowy orange from the effects of the TNT in the explosives. The factories themselves could be dangerous places to be. On 19 January 1917 in Silvertown in Essex, an explosion at a factory killed 73 people and injured more than 400. Thousands of local buildings were destroyed or damaged.

SOURCE C: Members of the Women's Land Army, 1918.

BOMBING

Airships were used by both sides to carry bombs. German **Zeppelins** were about 200 metres long and could carry 27 tons (24.5 metric tons) of bombs. Over 50 **bombing** raids were made over British towns, killing more than 1000 people. Civilians had become enemy targets in the latest development in warfare. German warships also launched shells at Hartlepool, Whitby and Scarborough in December 1914, causing significant damage to properties in the area.

SOURCE D: A German Zeppelin.

RATIONING – INTRODUCED IN 1918

The government was forced to introduce **rationing** because of the need to make food go further. Britain found it difficult to produce enough food to go around, and U-boats were preventing supplies getting through from abroad. Rationing was therefore introduced for any items or food stuffs that had to be imported – such as coffee, tea, chocolate or sugar.

DEFENCE OF THE REALM ACT

One of the first ways in which the country was changed was through the introduction of the Defence of the Realm Act (DORA) in August 1914. This was quite limiting in many respects. The Act did the following:

- prevented people communicating with the enemy or assisting them in any way
- secured the safety of home and allied forces
- prevented the spread of false reports
- introduced blackout in certain cities
- allowed the Press to be censored
- limited freedom of movement.

SOURCE E: The wreckage of a house after a Zeppelin raid.

✓ TASKS

1   Why was Britain known as the 'Home Front'?
2   Read **Source B**. How did the war change Mrs Felstead's life? What questions would you ask her if you could?
3   It took a while for women to gain the 'right to work' during the war. Why do you think this was? How important were women to the war effort once they were given this right?
4   What was the Silvertown explosion?
5   Using **Sources D** and **E** and the information given about bombing, write a short diary entry from the point of view of a teenager in his or her home during a Zeppelin raid. Make sure you explain what a Zeppelin is, and describe your thoughts and feelings.
6   a   What was the Defence of the Realm Act?
    b   What changes did it bring about in Britain?
7   You have been asked to produce a lesson for primary-school children on what life was like in Britain during the First World War. What would you include and why?

🔑 KEY WORDS

bombing
munitions
rationing
Zeppelins

👁 FINAL FOCUS

The First World War was especially significant for the lives of women. In 1918, for example, all women aged over 30 were given the vote as a reward for their efforts in the war. How do you think their lives changed after the war?

5.2 Reporting on the war

- Explain how the war was reported upon.
- Analyse the ways in which the war was reported upon.
- Judge how effective the methods of reporting were.

Today we are swamped by information in the media about what is going on in the world around us. This was not the case during the First World War, as newspaper reporting on warfare was still a relatively new idea. People could go to the cinema to see newsreels, but they did not have televisions in their homes. So how did they find out about what was going on in the war, and how successful were the methods of reporting?

KEY WORDS

censorship
propaganda
reporters

SOURCE A: War photography: these soldiers are out to get revenge for the death of a comrade. This picture is obviously staged. So what is the purpose of it?

 PEOPLE OF WWI

ENGLISH LADY EXECUTED IN BRUSSELS BY THE GERMANS FOR ASSISTING HER COUNTRYMEN

LONDON, Friday, 10.30pm.
The Foreign Office is informed by the United States Ambassador, that Miss Edith Cavell, lately head of a large training school for nurses at Brussels, who was arrested on August 5 last by the German authorities at that place, was executed on the 12th after sentence of death had been passed.

It is understood that the charge against Miss Cavell was that she had harboured fugitive British and French soldiers, and had assisted them to escape from Belgium, in order to join the colours.

SOURCE B: Edith Cavell's story as it appeared in the *Western Daily Press* on 16 October 1915.

REPORTING IN NEWSPAPERS

During the First World War, **reporters** wanted to give their readers the maximum amount of detail about the war. Newspapers provided a steady stream of information to the public, though they had to undergo **censorship**. Even as the death toll rose, newspapers motivated the public to support the war. One reporter, Sir Philip Gibbs, was given the sought-after opportunity of providing 'official' reports on the war. Gibbs was unwilling to be censored by the government at first, but he had to accept that they would not give him total freedom. Gibbs was serving alongside the troops on the Western Front, and was therefore able to report on the action.

One person whose death caused outrage when it was published in the newspapers was Edith Cavell, a nurse who was shot by the Germans (see **Source B**). The government was able to use her story as valuable **propaganda** to show the British public just what sort of people they were fighting against.

PUNCH MAGAZINE

A slightly less serious view on life in the war, both at the front and at home, was provided by *Punch* magazine, a collection of drawings and commentaries about what was going on. An extract from *Punch* can be seen in **Source C**.

PATHÉ'S ANIMATED GAZETTE

The First World War saw newspapers and magazines competing with film for the first time. One of these newsreels was produced by British Pathé and was called *Pathé's Animated Gazette*. It allowed people in Britain to view scenes from the war without having to be there themselves.

HOME-MADE MUNITIONS.

SOURCE C: A cartoon from *Punch* magazine entitled 'Homemade Munitions'. What do you think the message of this cartoon is?

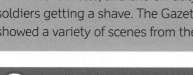

SOURCE D: The opening scene in Pathé's Animated Gazette, and two off-duty soldiers getting a shave. The Gazette showed a variety of scenes from the war.

👁 FINAL FOCUS

Reporting during the First World War, on both sides, was carefully controlled. How different would reporting have been if it revealed the true picture of suffering? What would the consequences have been?

✓ TASKS

1 a Who was Sir Philip Gibbs?
   b What does 'censorship' mean?
   c How did censorship affect reporters?

2 Look at **Source A**.
   a What is the photograph trying to show the British public?
   b Why are photographs like this not always the best sources of information?

3 Look at **Source B**.
   a What happened to Edith Cavell?
   b What sort of language is used in this article to draw people in?
   c Why do you think the media chose this particular story to focus upon?

4 What type of source is **Source C**? Who would this source have been popular with and why? Who would have disliked it?

5 Look at **Source D**.
   a How many people were these newsreels seen by?
   b What do you think was the purpose of the film showing the soldiers shaving?

6 Think carefully about **Sources A** to **D**. Decide which source is the best for informing us about the First World War, and write a paragraph explaining why. Make sure you refer to each of the sources.

6.1 A just and lasting peace?

OBJECTIVES

- Explain what the victorious nations wanted from the **Treaty of Versailles**.
- Describe what the Treaty of Versailles did to Germany.
- Judge how fair the Treaty of Versailles was.

SOURCE A: The 'Big Three' were the leaders of France, USA and Britain: (l to r) George Clemenceau, Woodrow Wilson and David Lloyd George.

STOP THE CLOCK

The Treaty of Versailles was signed on 28 June 1919, five years to the day after Archduke Franz Ferdinand was shot.

The First World War ended on 11 November 1918. Representatives from both sides met after the German **surrender**. The defeat was not sudden: German forces had been under pressure for a few months, after some successful allied advances on the Western Front. It had been a war that had seen both sides have the advantage at times, and both had been given plenty of opportunities to win. The outcome could have been very different. So what happened next? Could a lasting peace be achieved?

KEY WORDS

armistice
prisoner of war
surrender
treaty
Treaty of Versailles

TERMS OF SURRENDER

The leaders of the defeated powers agreed to stop fighting under certain conditions. These were laid out in an **armistice**, which they had to sign (see **Source C**). When Germany accepted the terms of surrender by signing the armistice there was much relief on behalf of Britain and its allies. The armistice was designed to significantly reduce the war supplies of the German armies.

SOURCE B: German **prisoners of war**.

Cessation of hostilities by land and in the air 6 hours after the signing of the Armistice.

Surrender in good condition by the German Armies of the following equipment:

- 5000 guns (2500 heavy, 2500 field).
- 25,000 machine guns.
- 3000 trench mortars.
- 1700 aeroplanes (fighters, bombers – firstly all D.7s and night-bombing machines).

5000 locomotives and 150,000 wagons, in good working order, with all necessary spare parts and fittings, shall be delivered to the Associated Powers.

SOURCE C: Some of the terms of the armistice of November 1918.

THE PARIS PEACE CONFERENCE

In the following year, 1919, the victorious nations met in Paris to discuss what to do with the defeated nations – but the defeated nations were not asked to attend. At this conference, five peace **treaties** were drawn up, the main one being the Treaty of Versailles. This Treaty dealt specifically with Germany, and the other powers were dealt with by the four other treaties.

The 'Big Three' – France, Britain and the USA – handled the most important decisions about Germany, but they all wanted different things from the Treaty with Germany. Coming to a compromise would not be easy. Would it be about revenge, a just and fair peace, or financial compensation? It would be a careful balancing act between punishing Germany too harshly, but at the same time making sure that Germany was punished enough so that they could not go to war again. The leaders of the countries had to decide whether or not they should:

- grind Germany into the ground
- take land and resources from Germany
- blame Germany entirely for the war
- give Germany a say in its punishment.

FINAL FOCUS

The Treaty was welcomed by some and criticized by others. Would you have done anything differently?

What did the Treaty of Versailles say?

- Germany should not be a part of the League of Nations (see p.56).
- Germany's army should have no more than 100,000 men.
- Germany should only have six battleships.
- Germany should have no air force.
- Germany should have no submarines.
- Germany should be allowed to have no 'Empire' or colonies.
- Germany must give up territory to the Allies (see **Source E**).
- Germany should accept total blame for the war.

SOURCE D: Some of the terms of the Treaty of Versailles.

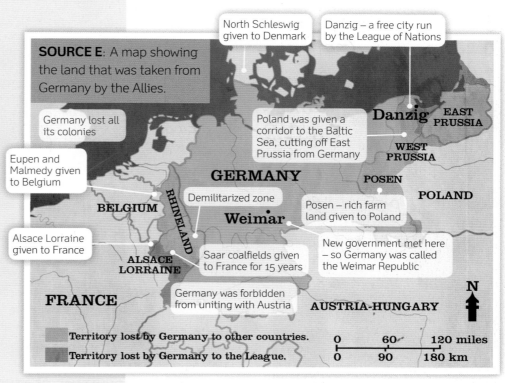

SOURCE E: A map showing the land that was taken from Germany by the Allies.

North Schleswig given to Denmark

Danzig – a free city run by the League of Nations

Germany lost all its colonies

Poland was given a corridor to the Baltic Sea, cutting off East Prussia from Germany

Eupen and Malmedy given to Belgium

Demilitarized zone

Posen – rich farm land given to Poland

Alsace Lorraine given to France

Saar coalfields given to France for 15 years

New government met here – so Germany was called the Weimar Republic

Germany was forbidden from uniting with Austria

DANZIG · EAST PRUSSIA · WEST PRUSSIA · POSEN · POLAND · GERMANY · Weimar · RHINELAND · BELGIUM · ALSACE LORRAINE · FRANCE · AUSTRIA-HUNGARY

Territory lost by Germany to other countries.
Territory lost by Germany to the League.

0   60   120 miles
0   90   180 km

N

TASKS

1 Look at the terms of the armistice in **Source C**.
   a How quickly was the fighting expected to end?
   b What did Germany have to give to the Allies?
2 What did the leaders of the victorious nations have to decide on? Why was it a difficult decision?
3 Think carefully: which leader was most likely to want revenge upon Germany: British, French or American? Explain your answer.
4 Look at what Germany was forced to accept in **Source D**. Put them in rank order from 1 to 8, and explain why you have made that decision.
5 Look at **Source E** and note down the territory that Germany lost. How would that make Germany feel?

GCSE-STYLE QUESTION

Explain why Germany saw the Treaty of Versailles as a harsh treaty.

6.2 Consequences

OBJECTIVES
- Describe some of the consequences of the First World War.
- Judge what the most significant consequence of the war was.

The Great War had wide-ranging consequences for the nations involved, some of which are more obvious than others. The most obvious consequence is that many people were killed or injured (see **Source B**). One unforeseen consequence was that France and Belgium were left with a huge clear-up operation to remove the bombs, bullets and trenches left behind by the war. Even today the debris of the Great War can still be found on the old battlefields. Other consequences had a huge impact on the remainder of the twentieth century.

SOURCE A: A significant consequence of the First World War was that European countries were changed or even created. A number of new countries were created bordering Russia, as land was taken from Germany. What countries can you see here?

KEY WORDS

communism
consequences
League of Nations
nationalism
revolution

STOP THE CLOCK

The First World War ended on 11 November 1918.

GRAPH SHOWING WARTIME DEATHS

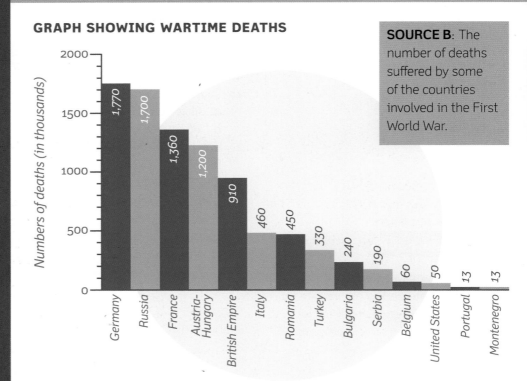

SOURCE B: The number of deaths suffered by some of the countries involved in the First World War.

THE END OF THE WAR
SOME IMPORTANT CONSEQUENCES

The USA began to rise as a major power in the world, as it still had a large army at the end of the war, and its factories and farms hadn't been damaged like those on the Western Front.

New, independent countries were formed meaning there was a growth of **nationalism**.

Dissatisfaction felt by the working classes in Russia because of limited rights, great poverty, and political disagreement, led to a **revolution** in Russia, and the growth of **communism**.

Because of the number of young British men who died during the war, around 2 million 'surplus women' of a certain age were left without a chance of getting married.

The cost of the war, in terms of finance as well as population, was high for many nations.

It was hoped that this war would be the war to end all wars, and the 'never again' mentality influenced Britain and its decision-making especially in the 1920s and 1930s.

The **League of Nations** was set up to keep the peace.

There was a huge amount of fear felt by the general public specifically in relation to air raids, as aircraft had greatly improved and caused many civilian casualties. Air raid shelters were improved and organizations such as Air Raid Precautions (ARP) were formed to manage risk.

Many nations had a desire for revenge – especially, but not only, Germany.

In nations such as Germany and Britain, working class men were given the right to vote, and many women were allowed to vote too.

Because of the scale of the movement of troops during the war, disease spread. An influenza epidemic in 1918 infected around 500 million people and is thought to have killed roughly 15% of that number.

There was a gradual end to the existence of empires.

FINAL FOCUS

The war had wide-ranging and varied consequences for all the nations that were involved. Do you think the world was a safer place after the First World War?

TASKS

1 Look at **Source B**.
   a How many people from Germany died in the First World War?
   b How many people from the British Empire died in the First World War?
   c Which nation lost the most men during the war?
2 Look at the list of consequences on this page.
   a Sort them into the following three categories: political, social, economic.
   b Now decide whether each consequence is likely to **keep the peace** in future, or whether it's likely to **lead to more war**.
3 Now sort all of the consequences into a list of importance, from most important to least important, and explain why you have made that decision. Do the whole class agree on what is the most important consequence of the First World War?

6.3 A Great War?

OBJECTIVES
* Describe the different ways in which the 'Great War' is remembered.
* Judge how the war should be remembered.

SOURCE A: Joyful crowds surge and cheer in victory celebrations in London, after the armistice.

History is full of different **interpretations** about events. People have their own ideas and opinions about how events happened and they should be remembered. The First World War is no different. It was a war of a scale and intensity that had never been seen before. Out of it came huge amounts of poetry, personal stories, art and photography. Historical collections are flooded with personal **remembrance**, and the war has served as the inspiration for many films, plays and television programmes. So how do we know what the First World War was really like?

NOW AND THEN

How the First World War is remembered today is quite different from how it was remembered in the years immediately after the war. Back then, the catastrophe was vivid in people's minds, and many thousands were grieving their lost loved ones (see **Source B**). However, alongside the grief was a great sense of relief: Britain and the Allies had won a great victory – and the four years of fighting, hard work and rationing was finally coming to an end (see **Source A**). Today, the First World War is marked every year on 11 November, and in Britain remembrance has become even more important in the wake of recent conflicts in Afghanistan and Iraq. We are much more aware of how many lives were lost, and the mistakes that were made by leaders of the army. However, First World War remembrance has arguably been skewed by personal stories which only convey a snapshot of the war. So how should the war be remembered?

SOURCE B: Soldiers carrying the coffin of an unknown soldier.

HOW SHOULD WE REMEMBER THE WAR?

We need to have a global perspective on the war – aggressive behaviour needs to be challenged, and the Allied troops were victorious in doing so.

We need to focus on personal stories – imagine what it must have been like to be orphaned or widowed. Thousands of people died like this unnecessarily.

We must focus on how the war changed the lives of individuals during and after the war: women were given opportunities to work, many were given the vote, and it marked the beginning of a new democratic era.

We should be very proud that we won the war. New inventions, clever strategies and excellently trained troops brought this about.

SOURCE C

✓ TASKS

1 a How is the First World War remembered today?
  b How was it remembered just after the war?
  c Why has the opinion changed?
2 What is an 'interpretation'? Write a short definition.
3 Look at **Sources A** and **B**. What does each one communicate about the First World War?
4 Look at **Source C**.
  a Put each comment in order from 1 to 4, where 1 is the most convincing argument for how we should remember the First World War, and 4 is the least convincing argument.
  b Explain to a partner why you made these choices.
5 Read **Source D**.
  a What is this poem about?
  b What is the mood of the poem?
  c What does it tell you about the First World War?
  d How useful is this source in providing a reliable picture of what the war was like? Explain your answer.
6 **Extension task**: Most families in Britain have been affected in some way by the First World War, for example loss of family members, or a significant change in profession or lifestyle. Can you find out anything about your own family history?

In Flanders fields the poppies blow
Between the crosses, row on row,
That mark our place; and in the sky
The larks, still bravely singing, fly
Scarce heard amid the guns below.

We are the Dead. Short days ago
We lived, felt dawn, saw sunset glow,
Loved and were loved, and now we lie
In Flanders fields.

Take up our quarrel with the foe:
To you from failing hands we throw
The torch; be yours to hold it high.
If ye break faith with us who die
We shall not sleep, though poppies grow
In Flanders fields.

SOURCE D: John McCrae's poem 'In Flanders Fields', May 1915, is one that comes from the heart, from despair about the death of a close friend and the subsequent funeral.

👁 FINAL FOCUS

It is very important to remember the beginning and the end of the First World War and all the associated events within its timeline. Should it be remembered as a great victory or a catastrophic loss of life?

Test your History skills

KNOWLEDGE AND UNDERSTANDING

1 Why did the war start?
2 How were people encouraged to join up to fight?
3 Which countries sent troops to support Britain?
4 Why did pilots get so famous?
5 State three problems that soldiers would face in the trenches.
6 What was meant by the term 'going over the top'?
7 How did the government control the content of letters that were sent home?
8 Why is the Battle of the Somme seen as a disaster?
9 Who led the British troops at the Battle of the Somme?
10 Name three new weapons that were used during the First World War.
11 Why was the 'war underground' so dangerous?
12 Name a famous pilot of the First World War.
13 What was a trench and why were they used?
14 How were the lives of women changed by the First World War?

INTERPRETATIONS

15 What interpretations exist about why the First World War started?
16 Should the 'boy soldiers' have been allowed to fight in the First World War?
17 Were the Generals of the First World War killing soldiers unnecessarily or were they simply trying to win a war?
18 Was the First World War a war of despair and needlessly lost lives, or a glorious victory?

CAUSATION

19 What were the short- and long-term causes of the First World War?

CHRONOLOGY

20 When did the First World War start and end?
21 When was the Battle of the Somme?
22 When did America enter the war and why?

SIGNIFICANCE

23 What was the most significant new invention of the war and why?
24 In your opinion, what was the most significant consequence of the war?
25 In terms of our memory and interpretations of the First World War, what topic that you have studied was the most significant and why?

EXTENDED WRITING

26 Many people believe that we should always remember the First World War. Do you agree? Why, or why not?

PROJECT TASK

27 Using this book and the films from the Pathé archive, create a project on a topic of your choice. Your project could be in the form of:
  a A storyboard for a historical film
  b A presentation
  c A piece of extended writing.

Assessment

Task: *How useful are Sources A – C to a historian studying what life was like in the trenches? Write three paragraphs and refer to your own knowledge. (8 marks)*

I always said a prayer before going over the top ... I'll never forget it. 'Dear God, I am going into grave danger. Please help me to act like a man and come back safe.' And that's what I did. And I went over without fear. That little prayer seemed to save my life because I had no fear left, although there were shells and bullets and all the rest flying when we went over and I were never frightened of being hit ... And six times I went up and six times I said that little prayer and each time I went up and come back safe. And I thank God for it.

SOURCE A: Arthur Barraclough speaking about his experiences of 'going over the top' and how he believed his faith kept him safe.

Despite all the rain, there was little fresh water in the front line as everything we needed had to be carried up. Ration parties would bring the water up in petrol cans which were rarely washed out. ... Washing was almost impossible. Behind the support lines, if you were lucky, you might find an old shell hole where the mud had gradually settled, and the top of the water being reasonably clear, you could get a wash in that.

SOURCE B: A historian writing with the help of insights from Harry Patch, a war veteran, in *The Last Fighting Tommy*, 2008.

The latrine arrangements were pretty primitive ... the army set aside an area of grass field at the edge of the village where the pioneer or sanitary men dug a dozen little trenches, three feet long by one foot wide and about three feet deep, and without any canvas sacking or anything to hide the view, one dropped one's trousers, bestrode a trench, crouched and attended to nature.

SOURCE C: A description of a trench latrine by modern historian Neil Hanson, in *The Unknown Soldier: The Story of the Great War*, 2007.

WRITING YOUR ANSWER

In order to answer this question, you'll need to make sure you have addressed the following questions for each source:

- Why is this source useful?
- Why is this particular author useful?
- Does this source agree with my own knowledge of the trenches?
- What is left out of the source, and how would this make it more useful?
- Overall, how useful is it?

ASSESSING YOUR WORK

Use this grid to assess your own work. How can you improve it?

Marks	Criteria
1–2	Understand and describe the information in the sources.
3–4	Describe and explain in basic terms why the sources are useful.
5–6	Identify the differences between the origins of the sources and evaluate their usefulness.
7–8	Make a considered judgment about the reliability of each source and compare their usefulness.

Glossary

absolute Total

Ace Expert

aircraft Plane or airship

alliance Team

alternative Another option or choice

ANZAC Australian and New Zealand Army Corps

armistice Agreement reached; surrender

assassination Killing

battlefields Areas where battles took place

bayonet Knife or blade fixed on the end of a gun

biplane Double-winged aircraft with an open cockpit

Black Hand gang Serbian terrorist group

bombardment Heavy, continuous bombing

bombing Dropping bombs or shells on the enemy

bravery Showing great courage

British Empire Collection of countries under British control

British Expeditionary Force The professional British army in 1914

celebration Congratulations and rejoicing

censorship Removing information from a document

chlorine Chemical gas or liquid, often found in household cleaners

clay-kicker Term used to describe a miner or tunneller

colonies Countries controlled by another country as part of their empire

combat Fighting

Commonwealth What is left of the British Empire after some nations were given independence

communism A system of social organization where all property is owned by the community and each person contributes according to their ability

conscientious objector Somebody who objects to fighting

conscription Forced joining of the armed forces

consequences Results

convoy Procession; line

court martial Military court case

coward Somebody who is not brave

Dardanelles a narrow passage in Turkey which connects the Aegean Sea to the Sea of Marmara

Dead Man's Penny Plaque sent to the family of a dead soldier

deserter Somebody who leaves their 'post' in the armed forces without permission

dog fight Fight in the air between planes

duckboard Wooden board on the floor of a trench

dugout Shelter dug into the soil in a trench

faith Trust in somebody or something

fear Feeling afraid

fire bay Section cut out of a trench to shelter soldiers from gun fire

fire step Soldiers would stand on this to shoot a gun out of the trench

global Worldwide

grenade Bomb that is thrown by hand

hindsight The ability to 'look back' and make a balanced judgment

Home Front Where the events of WWI had an impact 'back home' in Britain, such as air raids

imperialism The desire to have the best collection of countries and to be the richest.

incentive Something that encourages someone to perform an action

interpretation A historical opinion

latrine Toilet

League of Nations Established as part of the Treaty of Versailles; a group of countries who agreed to protect each other

lice Small parasite that causes itching

long-term cause A cause from longer than ten years ago

memorial Something in memory of somebody

militarism The desire to have the biggest and best army and navy

mole Small, burrowing animal

mobilize To get your armed forces ready for war

munitions Bombs, guns, bullets; anything connected with fighting with weapons

mutiny Disobeying orders or commanding officers

nationalism The desire to be a country that is able to make decisions about what they do and when they do it

navy Ships and submarines

neutral Not taking a particular side

No Man's Land Area between the trenches

opinion Point of view

Ottoman Turkish

pacifist Believes in peaceful methods

Pals Battalion Battalion made up of friends or colleagues

pardon To forgive

phosgene Type of gas used in the First World War

plastic surgery Operations to correct injuries or deformities

posthumous Occurring after a person's death

prisoners of war People taken prisoner by the enemy

projector Extend outwards

propaganda Promoting a particular point of view through the use of the media

prospect Idea; possibility

rationing Making food and resources go further by limiting the amount that people can have

rations A person's allowance during rationing

reconnaissance Watching out for events and activities by the enemy

recruitment Getting people to join up

reporter Somebody who collects information to let people know what is happening

requirements What is needed

restrictions What cannot be done, or is not permitted

revolution An overthrow of a government or social order

Roses of No Man's Land Nurses on the 'Front line'

Schlieffen Plan Germany's battle plan to defeat France and then Russia in WWI

shell shock Psychological effects of war

shipping Boats

short-term cause A cause from within the last five to ten years

shrapnel Metal splinters or ball-bearings from a bomb

sloop Ship

stalemate When neither side can win

stand to Morning ritual in the trenches; soldiers get ready for the day ahead

supply To provide

surrender Give up

trauma An injury, either physical or mental

trawler A fishing boat that drags nets behind it

treaty Signed agreement

Treaty of Versailles Agreement signed in 1919 between the Germans and the victorious nations

trench Long, thin hole in the ground

trench foot Feet 'rotting' due to being constantly cold and wet

trench raids Attacking an enemy trench

trigger Pulling this fires a gun

troops Soldiers

U-boat Submarine

underage Too young for something

Victoria Cross Medal; the highest military honour for bravery

volunteer Somebody who wants to do something unpaid

Western Front The line of trenches from the sea to Switzerland, west of Germany, where fighting took place in WWI – these were in France and Belgium

White Feather Campaign Campaign by women to give a white feather to men who they thought were cowardly for not joining up

Zeppelin Airship

Index

Where a subject has several page numbers, the ones in **bold** contain the main information.